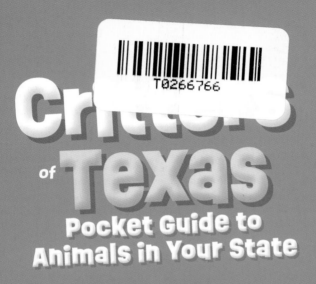

Critters
of Texas

Pocket Guide to
Animals in Your State

ALEX
TROUTMAN

produced in cooperation with
Wildlife Forever

PUBLICATIONS
Adventure
an imprint of AdventureKEEN

About Wildlife Forever

Wildlife Forever works to conserve America's outdoor heritage through conservation education, preservation of habitat, and scientific management of fish and wildlife. Wildlife Forever is a 501c3 nonprofit organization dedicated to restoring habitat and teaching the next generation about conservation. Become a member and learn more about innovative programs like the Art of Conservation®, The Fish and Songbird Art Contests®, Clean Drain Dry Initiative™, and Prairie City USA®. For more information, visit wildlifeforever.org.

Thank you to Ann McCarthy, the original creator of the Critters series, for her dedication to wildlife conservation and to environmental education. Ann dedicates her work to her daughters, Megan and Katharine Anderson

Front cover photos by **Chris Desborough/shutterstock.com:** pronghorn, **Matt Jeppson/shutterstock.com:** Texas horned lizard, **Brian Lasenby/shutterstock.com:** scissor-tailed flycatcher
Back cover photo by **Jeff W. Jarrett/Shutterstock.com:** Texas toad

Edited by Brett Ortler and Jenna Barron
Cover and book design by Jonathan Norberg
Proofreader: Emily Beaumont

10 9 8 7 6 5 4 3 2 1

Critters of Texas
First Edition 2004, Second Edition 2024
Copyright © 2004 by Wildlife Forever, Copyright © 2024 by Alex Troutman
The first edition (2004) of this book was produced by Wildlife Forever.
AdventureKEEN is grateful for its continued partnership and advocacy on behalf of the natural world.

Published by Adventure Publications
An imprint of AdventureKEEN
310 Garfield Street South, Cambridge, Minnesota 55008
(800) 678-7006
www.adventurepublications.net
All rights reserved
Printed in China
Cataloging-in-Publication data is available from the Library of Congress
ISBN 978-1-64755-464-4 (pbk.); 978-1-64755-465-1 (ebook)

Acknowledgments

I want to thank everyone who believed in and supported me over the years—a host of friends, family, and teachers. I want to especially thank my mom and my siblings Van, Bre, and TJ.

Dedication

I dedicate this book to my brother Van:
May you continue to enjoy the birds and wildlife in heaven.

This book is for all the kids who have a passion for nature and the outdoors, especially ones who identify as Black, Brown, Indigenous, and People of Color. May this be an encouragement to never give up. And if you have a dream and passion for something, pursue it relentlessly. I also hope to set an example that you can be successful as your full, authentic self!

Lastly, I dedicate this book to all those with ADHD and dyslexia, as well as all other members of the neurodivergent community. While our quirks make things more challenging, our goals are not impossible to reach; sometimes it takes a little more time and help, but we, too, can succeed!

Contents

Reptiles and Amphibians

Introduction

My passion for nature started when I was young. I was always amazed by the sunlit fiery glow of the red-tailed hawks as they soared overhead when I went fishing with my family. The red-tailed hawk was my spark bird—the bird that captures your attention and gets you into birding. Through my many encounters with red-tailed hawks, and other species like garter snakes and coyotes, I found a passion for nature and the environment. Stumbling across conservationists like Steve Irwin, Jeff Corwin, and Jack Hanna introduced me to the field of Wildlife Biology as a career and gave birth to a dream that I was able to accomplish an live out: serving as a Fish and Wildlife Biologist for governmental agencies, as well as in the private sector.

My childhood dream was driven by a desire to learn more about the different types of ecosystems and the animals that call our wil places home. Books and field guides like this one whet my thirst for knowledge. Even before I could fully understand the words on the pages, I was drawn to books and flashcards that had animals on them. I could soon identify every animal I was shown and tell fact about it. I hope that this edition of *Critters of Texas* can be the fuel that sustains your passion for not only learning about wildlife but also for caring for the environment and making sure that all a welcome in the outdoors. For others, may this book be the spark that ignites a flame for wildlife preservation and environmental stewardship. I hope that this book inspires children from lower socioeconomic and minority backgrounds to pursue their dreams to the fullest and be unapologetically themselves.

By profession, I'm a Fish and Wildlife Biologist, and I'm a nature enthusiast through and through. My love for nature includes making sure that everyone has an equal opportunity to enjoy the outdoors in their own way. So, as you use this book, I encourage you to be intentional in inviting others to appreciate nature with you. Enjoy your discoveries and stay curious!

–Alex Troutma

Texas: The Lone Star State

Texas is known for its open skies, diverse landscapes, cowboy culture, and, of course, the Alamo (don't forget it!). The Spanish settlers first came to Texas as missionaries, and many wars were fought for the land before it officially became a state in 1845. But long before then, it was home to Comanche, Akokisa, Karankawa, Mogollon, and other Native American tribes. The name Texas came from the Caddo tribe's word for "friends," which is why the state motto is simply "friendship." It is also called the Lone Star State because it was the Republic of Texas before it was a state; the state flag has a single star on it to show its independence.

Texas is the second largest state (after Alaska) and has many different natural landscapes. It touches the Gulf of Mexico on the southeast, as well as the Pine Belt where a lot of commercial timber grows. Above that in the northeast is where more of the state's ranches and farmlands are. The Great Plains takes up the northern part of Texas. Far west is a huge shift in landscape, going from flat land to a mountainous region. Finally in the south is the Rio Grande, which is a long river that borders Mexico.

These environments are home to many animals, including 140-plus species of mammals, more than 600 species of birds (the most in the United States), and 231 species of reptiles and amphibians, not to mention fish, countless insects and spiders, plants, and more. This is your guide to the animals, birds, reptiles, and amphibians that call Texas home.

Some of Texas's most iconic plants, animals, and other natural resources are now officially recognized as state symbols. Get to know them below and see if you can spot them all! You'll probably encounter the state nickname and motto, so I've included them here too.

State Bird:
northern
mockingbird

State Cactus:
prickly pear
cactus

State Tree:
pecan tree

State Flower:
bluebonnet

State Fish:
Guadalupe
bass

State Amphibian:
Texas toad

State Reptile:
Texas horned lizard

State Mammal:
Texas longhorn

**State
Nickname:**
The Lone
Star State

State Butterfly:
monarch
butterfly

State Motto:
"Friendship"

How to Use This Guide

This book is your introduction to some of the wonderful critters found in Texas; it includes 23 mammals, 24 birds, and 18 reptiles and amphibians. It includes some animals you probably already know, such as northern raccoons and bald eagles, but others you may not know about, such as speckled kingsnakes or crested caracaras. I've selected the species in this book because they are widespread (coyotes, page 24), abundant (white-tailed deer, page 56), or well-known, but best observed from a safe distance (western diamondback rattlesnake, page 134).

The book is organized by types of animals: mammals, birds, and reptiles and amphibians. Within each section, the animals are in alphabetical order. If you'd like to look for a critter quickly, turn to the checklist (page 140), which you can also use to keep track of how many animals you've seen! For each species, you'll see a photo of the animal, along with neat facts and information on the animal's habitat, diet, its predators, how it raises its young, and more.

Safety Note

Nature can be unpredictable, so don't go outdoors alone, and always tell an adult when you're going outside. All wild animals should be treated with respect. If you see one—big or small—don't get close to it or attempt to touch or feed it. Instead, keep your distance and enjoy spotting it. If you can, snap some pictures with a camera or make a quick drawing using a sketchbook. If the animal is getting too close, is acting strangely, or seems sick or injured, tell an adult right away, as it might have rabies, a disease that can affect mammals. The good news is there's a rabies vaccine, so it's important to visit a doctor right away if you get bit or scratched by a wild animal.

Notes About Icons

Each species page includes basic information about an animal, from what it eats to how it survives the winter. The book also includes information that's neat to know; in the mammals section, each page includes a simple track illustration of the animal, with approximate track size included. And along the bottom, there is an example track pattern for the mammal, with the exception for those that primarily glide or fly (flying squirrels and bats).

On the left-hand page for each mammal, a rough-size illustration is included that shows how big the animal is when compared to a basketball.

Also on the left-hand page, there are icons that tell you when each animal is most active: nocturnal (at night), diurnal (during the day), or crepuscular (at dawn/dusk), so you know when to look. If an animal has a "zzz" icon, it hibernates during the winter. Some animals hibernate every winter, and their internal processes (breathing and heartbeat) slow down almost entirely. Other animals only partially hibernate, but this still helps them save energy and survive through the coldest part of the year.

nocturnal
(active at night)

diurnal
(active during day)

crepuscular
(most active at
dawn and dusk)

hibernates/deep sleeper
(dormant during winter)

ground nest   cup nest   platform nest   cavity nest   migrates

On the left-hand side of each bird page, the nest for the species is shown, along with information on whether or not the bird migrates; on the right-hand side, there's information on where it goes.

Did you know?

Badgers are solitary animals, but they will sometimes hunt with coyotes in a team. A coyote will chase prey into the badger's den, and the badger will chase or dig out the prey that coyotes like. The badger's den has one entrance with a pile of dirt next to it. When a badger is threatened, it will back into its burrow and show its teeth.

Size Comparison	Most Active	Track Size	Hibernates
		2¾"	

American Badger

Taxidea taxus

Size: 2–3 feet long; weighs 8–25 pounds

Habitat: Savannas, grasslands, and meadows

Range: Can be found throughout the Midwest and westward through the Great Plains to the western coast of the United States and southward into Mexico. In Texas, they are found throughout, except for the farthest eastern portion of the state.

Food: Carnivores, they eat pocket gophers, moles, ground squirrels, and other rodents. They will also eat dead animals (or carrion), fish, reptiles, and a few types of birds, especially ground-nesting birds.

Den: Badgers are fossorial (a digging animal that spends a lot of time underground); they build many dens or burrows throughout their range. Most dens are used to store food, but badgers also use dens to sleep in and raise their young. Dens can be over 10 feet deep and 4 feet wide.

Young: Cubs are born, with eyes closed, usually in April or May in litters of 2–3. Extensive care is provided by the mom for up to 3 months. After another 2–3 months, the young will gain their independence.

Predators: Bears, bobcats, mountain lions, coyotes, golden eagles, and humans

Tracks: The front tracks are 2¾ inches long and 2 inches wide.

The American badger is a short, bulky mammal with grayish to dirty-red fur. Badgers have a distinctive face with a series of cream-and-white stripes offset by a black background.

Did you know?

Beavers are rodents! Yes, these flat-tailed mammals are rodents, like rats and squirrels. In fact, they are the largest native rodents in North America. Just like other rodents, beavers have large incisors, which they use to chew through trees to build dams and dens. Beavers are the original wetland engineers. By damming rivers and streams, beavers create ponds and wetlands.

Size Comparison Most Active Track Size

American Beaver

Castor canadensis

Size: Body is 25–30 inches long; tail is 9–13 inches long; weighs 30–70 pounds

Habitat: Wooded wetland areas near ponds, streams, and lakes

Range: Beavers can be found throughout Texas, as well as much of the rest of the US.

Food: Leaves, twigs, and stems; they also feed on fruits and aquatic plant roots. Throughout the year they gather and store tree cuttings, which they eat in winter.

Den: A beaver's home is called a lodge. It consists of a pile of branches that is splattered with mud and vegetation. Lodges are constructed on the banks of lakes and streams and have exits and entrances that are underwater.

Young: Young beavers (kits) are born in late April through May and June in litters of 3–4. After two years they are considered mature and will be forced out of the den.

Predators: Bobcats, mountain lions, bears, wolves, and coyotes. Human trappers are major predators too.

Tracks: A beaver's front foot looks a lot like your hand; it has five fingers. The hind (back) foot is long, with five separate toes that have webbing or extra skin between them.

Beavers range from dark brown to reddish brown. They have a stocky body with hind legs that are longer than the front legs. The beaver's body is covered in dense fur, but its tail is naked and has special blood vessels that help it cool or warm its body.

Did you know?

Female bears weigh between 90 and 300 pounds and are smaller than the average adult human male in the US. But don't let their small size fool you; with a bite force around 800 pounds per square inch (PSI) and swiping force of over 400 pounds, these bears are not to be taken lightly.

Size Comparison Most Active Track Size Hibernates

6–7"

16

Black Bear

Ursus americanus

Size: 5–6 feet long (nose to tail); weighs 90–600 pounds

Habitat: Forests, lowland areas, and swamps

Range: Black bears can be found in many parts of North America, from Alaska down through Canada and into Mexico. In Texas, they are found throughout the southwestern corner of the state.

Food: Berries, fish, seeded crops, small mammals, wild grapes, tree shoots, ants, bees, beavers, and even deer fawns

Den: Denning usually starts in December, with bears emerging in late March or April. Dens can be either dug (out of a hillside, for example) or constructed with materials such as leaves, grass, and moss.

Young: Two cubs are usually born at one time (a litter), often in January. Cubs are born without fur and blind, with pink skin. They weigh 8–16 ounces.

Predators: Humans and other bears. Sometimes, other carnivores, such as mountain lions, wolves, coyotes, or even bobcats, will prey on black bears. Cubs are especially vulnerable.

Tracks: Front print is usually 4–6 inches long and 3½–5 inches wide, with the hind foot being 6–7 inches long and 3½–5 inches wide. The feet have five toes.

Black bears are usually black in color, but they can be many different variations of black and brown. Some even have grayish, reddish, or blonde fur.

Did you know?

Black-tailed jackrabbits are hares, not rabbits. The difference is that rabbits are smaller and born without fur, while hares are larger and born with fur. Jackrabbits have powerful legs that allow them to reach speeds of over 30 miles per hour and leap more than 10 feet in length.

Size Comparison

Most Active

Track Size

2½—5½"

Black-tailed Jackrabbit

Lepus californicus

Size: 2 feet long; weighs 3–9 pounds

Habitat: Brushlands, desert scrublands, farmlands, prairies, and meadows

Range: They can be found in the western United States from southern Washington into California and as far east as Nebraska and Texas. In Texas, they can be found almost statewide, except in the easternmost area of the state.

Food: Jackrabbits are herbivores that mainly eat plants like alfalfa and clover. In the fall and winter months, they will also eat woody vegetation.

Den: No den; bunnies are born in scratched-out, hollow depressions.

Young: Bunnies are born at around 40 days after pregnancy. They are born with hair and are active soon after birth. Young nurse for only a few days and reach reproductive maturity within their first year.

Predators: Coyotes, foxes, bobcats, badgers, and weasels

Tracks: Front feet are around 2–2½ inches long and 1¼–1¾ inches wide. Hind feet are 2½–5½ inches long and around 1½–2½ inches wide.

The black-tailed jackrabbit is a large, long-eared hare. It has dark, peppery-brown fur and black-tipped ears. The black-tailed jackrabbit has very long front and rear legs. It has a black stripe that runs down its back. Males and females look alike, but females are usually larger.

Did you know?

Even though they are called prairie dogs, they are not in the canine or dog family; they are actually rodents belonging to the squirrel family. The black-tailed is the most common of the prairie dog species. Prairie dogs use a variety of vocalizations to communicate. They will even "bark" to alert others to danger.

Size Comparison   Most Active   Track Size

   1–2"

Black-tailed Prairie Dog

Cynomys ludovicianus

Size: 14–17 inches long; weighs 2–3 pounds

Habitat: Grassy plains and prairies

Range: They are found in the Great Plains east of the Rocky Mountains and into Mexico. In Texas, they can be found in the central and northwestern portion of the state.

Food: Grasses, seeds, plants, and sometimes insects

Den: They live in multi-burrow colonies called "towns." Burrows can be 3–6 feet wide, sometimes as deep as 15 feet underground, and have several chambers. The nest chamber is usually lined with grass.

Young: One litter of 3–5 pups is born after 30–35 days of pregnancy. Pups are born hairless and blind. They open their eyes around 5 weeks and will start exploring outside the burrow around the same time. Both parents care for young and, once they are aboveground, any female producing milk will nurse them. They will leave the coterie (group of prairie dogs) at 1 year old.

Predators: Black-footed ferrets are their main predators; snakes, eagles, coyotes, hawks, falcons, and badgers.

Tracks: The front foot is 1–1½ inches long and hind foot is 1–2 inches long. Both sets are ⅞–1⅜ inches wide with claw marks at the end of each toe.

Prairie dogs come in various shades of brown and tan. They have small, thick bodies; rounded ears; a short tail; sharp teeth; and strong claws for digging. Their tail is black at the tip, hence their name.

21

Did you know?

Collared peccaries are not pigs! In fact, they do not share any recent ancestors. One way to distinguish them is that collared peccaries' tails are stumped and not easily visible, while pigs' tails are long. Also, collared peccaries have a scent gland on the top of their rump, while pigs do not. They will use this gland to rub their scent on trees and rocks to mark territory.

Size Comparison   Most Active   Track Size

1¼"

22

Collared Peccary

Pecari tacaju

Size: 14–17 inches long; weighs 2–3 pounds

Habitat: Brush country, grasslands, woodlands, and semi-desert rocky canyons

Range: They can be found from southwestern Texas down into Central America and as far south as Argentina.

Food: They feed on various cacti, fruits, other types of vegetation, insects, and sometimes snakes.

Den: They have no permanent nests or dens but lie down as a group in grassy areas.

Young: Usually 2 young are born per litter after a pregnancy of almost 5 months. The young have a reddish or yellow hue. Young are sometimes called "reds" because of the color of their hair. They are able explore with their mom a few days after birth. Males become reproductively mature at around 46–47 weeks and females at around 33–34 weeks.

Predators: Mountain lions, humans, coyotes, bobcats, and jaguars

Tracks: The front feet have four hoofed toes, and the hind feet have three, though only two toe prints are noticeable.

Collared peccaries look like small, hairy pigs, minus a tail. They have a white-to-cream-colored collar on top of a black coarse-coated body. The white collar is where they get their name. Females and males look the same. They have small eyes, large heads, and straight canine teeth or tusks on both the top and bottom jaws.

23

Did you know?

At one time, coyotes were only found in the central and western parts of the US, but now, with the help of humans (eliminating predators and clearing forests), they can be found throughout most of the country.

Size Comparison

Most Active

Track Size

2"

Coyote

Canis latrans

Size: 3–4 feet long; weighs 21–50 pounds

Habitat: Urban and suburban areas, woodlands, grasslands, and farm fields

Range: Coyotes can be found in all the counties of Texas. They are also found throughout the US and Mexico, the northern parts of Central America, and in southern Canada.

Food: A variety of prey, including rodents, birds, deer, and sometimes livestock

Den: Coyotes will dig their own dens but will often use old fox or badger dens or hollow logs.

Young: 5–7 pups, independent around 8–10 months

Predators: Bears and wolves; humans trap and kill for pelts and to "protect" livestock.

Tracks: Four toes and a carpal pad (the single pad below the toe pads) can be seen on all four feet.

Coyotes have brown, reddish-brown, or gray back fur with a lighter gray-to-white belly. They have a longer muzzle than other wild canines. They are active mostly during the night (nocturnal) but also during the twilight and dawn hours (crepuscular).

Did you know?

The largest wild sheep in North America is the bighorn sheep. Their horns can be over 3 feet long, as thick as 1 foot, and can weigh over 20 pounds. Bighorn sheep are agile, able to run over 30 miles per hour and jump over 19 feet from one ledge to another.

Size Comparison   Most Active   Track Size

   2½—3½"

Desert Bighorn Sheep

Ovis canadensis nelsoni

Size: 5–6 feet long; weighs 125–200 pounds or more

Habitat: Alpine meadows; grassy mountain slopes; and foothill country close to rugged, rocky cliffs and bluffs

Range: They can be found in Arizona, southern California, Utah, New Mexico, and Texas. After reintroduction in Texas, they can be found in the western part of the state.

Food: Grasses, clovers, sedges, and flowers

Den: No den

Young: One lamb is born around 150–180 days after breeding. Young are precocial, meaning they are able to walk and stand a few minutes to hours after birth. By months 4–6, lambs are weaned. During the first year of life, they learn their home territory. Males will leave their mom at 2–4 years old to join a male group, and females will usually stay with their mom for life.

Predators: Wolves, coyotes, golden eagles, bears, and mountain lions

Tracks: Front and hind tracks are 2½–3½ inches long and 1¾–2½ inches wide.

Both male and female bighorn sheep have light-to-dark-brown fur; they sometimes have a grayish hue. Their muzzle, backs of legs, and rump are white. The males (rams) have large, circular horns that frame their face. Females (ewes, pronounced like "yous") have shorter horns that are not as circular. Young (lambs) are grayish with a blackish-brown tail.

Did you know?

The eastern fox squirrel's bones appear pink under ultraviolet (UV) light, a type of light human eyes can't see. Squirrels accidentally help plant trees by forgetting where they have previously buried nuts. Sometimes, they seem to pretend to bury nuts to throw off would-be nut thieves.

Size Comparison   Most Active   Track Size

2½"

Eastern Fox Squirrel

Sciurus niger

Size: 19–28 inches long; weighs 1–3 pounds

Habitat: Open woodlands, suburban areas, and dense forests

Range: They are found throughout much of Texas, except the northwestern parts of the state. They are found in the eastern United States to Texas and as far north as the Dakotas.

Food: Acorns, seeds, nuts, insects such as moths and beetles, birds, eggs, and dead fish

Den: Ball-shaped dreys, or nests, are made of vegetation like leaves, sometimes in tree cavities.

Young: 2–3 kits are born between December and February and May and June. Kittens are born naked and weigh half an ounce; they are cared for by their parents for the first 7–8 weeks. They can reproduce by around 10–11 months for males and 8 months for females.

Predators: Humans, hawks, cats, coyotes, bobcats, and weasels

Tracks: The front tracks have four digits (toes), and the hind feet have five digits.

The eastern fox squirrel is the largest tree squirrel in Texas. It is gray or reddish brown with a yellowish or light-brown underside. There is also a rare black and smoky-gray phases. Both the male and female look the same.

Did you know?

Mexican free-tailed bats are the fastest-known mammals on Earth, even faster than a cheetah at over 99 miles per hour (mph). A colony of Mexican free-tailed bats can consume over 250 tons of insects in a night; this makes them great at pest control for farmers. Sometimes they fly over 10,000 feet high. They get their name from the little section of tail that sticks out from their skin.

Size Comparison   Most Active

Mexican Free-tailed Bat

Tadarida brasiliensis

Size: 3–4 inches long; wingspan is 11–12 inches; weighs ¼–½ ounce

Habitat: Wetland areas, caves, suburban areas, urban areas, forests, and deserts

Range: They are found across Texas, as well as throughout most of the southern half of the US.

Food: Carnivores; moths, beetles, flies, and dragonflies

Den: Roost sites are usually near water and in caves. Human structures like bridges, abandoned buildings, and mines are also used. Bats nest in colonies from as few as 40 bats to up to several thousand.

Young: One pup is born 11–12 weeks after mating. Pups roost in high areas where it is hot. Pups are raised by females. In about 4–7 weeks, they are independent. They can reproduce at around 9 months for females and 2 years for males.

Predators: Barn owls, red-tailed hawks, skunks, opossums, raccoons, and snakes

Tracks: Though they are rarely on the ground to leave a track, it would show one thumbprint from the forearm and a hind footprint.

The Mexican free-tailed bat is also known as the Brazilian free-tailed bat. Mexican free-tailed bats are medium-size bats. They are dark brown to clay-red in color. They have large ears with black tips, a short nose, and wrinkled lips. They have long, narrow wings and a small, exposed tail.

Did you know?

The Mexican long-nosed bat has a long tongue that extends almost 3 inches outside of its mouth (almost as long as its body). They follow the flowering and fruiting cycles of their food; this makes them have one of the longest migrations for bats. They are the largest species of nectar-eating bats in the Americas.

Size Comparison   Most Active

Mexican Long-nosed Bat

Leptonycteris nivalis

Size: 2¾–3½ inches long; wingspan of 14 inches; weighs ½–1 ounce

Habitat: Old mines, caves, cliff-face cavities, urban areas, forests, and deserts and desert scrublands

Range: During the summer months of June–August, they are found in California, Texas, Arizona, and New Mexico. In Texas, they are found in the southern tip bordering Mexico.

Food: They feed on nectar from various types of agave plants, cacti, and fruit; they will sometimes eat insects.

Den: Roost sites are in caves or human structures like abandoned buildings and mines. Bats nest in colonies of as few as 40 bats up to several thousand.

Young: One pup is born per year; the female will carry it during flights until it is weaned and can fly on its own, which is usually a couple of months after birth.

Predators: Owls, bobcats, and snakes

Tracks: Though they are rarely on the ground to leave a track, they have a thumbprint on their forearm and a hind footprint.

The Mexican long-nosed bat is also known as the greater long-nosed bat. It is gray to brown on its upper body, and the underbody is lighter. It has darker fur that is fluffier than that of other bat species. Fur tips are sliver and white at the base (closest to the body). They have a short tail and a long muzzle or snout.

Did you know?

Mountain lions are the second-largest cat in the western part of the world. The largest is the jaguar. Mountain lions do not roar like other big cats, but rather they scream! They also make other sounds similar to pet cats, like hissing and purring. Mountain lions can jump as high as 18 feet off the ground into a tree.

Size Comparison   Most Active   Track Size

3"

Mountain Lion

Puma concolor

Size: 6–8 feet long; weighs 100–154 pounds

Habitat: Grasslands, deserts, wetlands, shrublands, forests, swamps, and upland forests

Range: They can be seen from northern Canada to Argentina. In Texas, they are mostly found in the western Trans-Pecos and southern bushland regions.

Food: Deer, wild boars, raccoons, birds, rabbits, mice, and occasionally livestock

Den: Will den in caves, rock piles and crevices, and thickets. Dens are usually lined with plants.

Young: 1–6 kittens are born with spots almost 100 days after mating. Weaning takes place around day 4, and the young kits will stay with their mom another year or two. Spots fade at around 6 months. Males reach reproductive maturity at around 3 years old and females around 2½ years, though they usually do not reproduce until they have a permanent home territory.

Predators: No natural predators, but they will sometimes get in territory disputes with other large carnivores.

Tracks: Front tracks are 3¼ inches long and wide. The back or hind tracks are 3 inches long and wide.

Mountain lion fur is golden tan to dusky brown on the back; its underside is a pale buff color with a white throat and chest area. They have a pink nose, black ear tips, and a smoky gray-black muzzle. The tip of their tail is black like their ears, and their eyes are brown. Their tail is long and makes up a third of their body length. Kittens have spots and smoky-blue eyes.

Did you know?

The armadillo is the state small mammal of Texas. There are around 20 species of armadillos, but the nine-banded is the only one found in the United States. Though they are called the nine-banded armadillo, they can have as few as 7 bands or as many as 11! Armadillo translates from Spanish to mean "little armored one."

Size Comparison   Most Active   Track Size

2"

Nine-banded Armadillo

Dasypus novemcinctus

Size: 15–17 inches long; weighs 9–17 pounds

Habitat: Scrublands, grasslands, woody areas, swamps and salt marshes, and forests

Range: They have a range from South America to North America. They are found in all but the western corner of Texas.

Food: Ants, wasps, beetles, grubs, spiders, scorpions, snails, and eggs of various animals

Den: They use burrows that are dug or reuse burrows abandoned by other armadillos.

Young: With only one litter per year, they give birth to four identical quadruplets. Young are born closely resembling adults but smaller. Their eyes open quickly, but their leathery skin does not harden into its characteristic armor for a few weeks. Young of both sexes reach full reproductive maturity at 2 years.

Predators: Coyotes, bobcats, raptors, alligators, and mountain lions

Tracks: Front tracks are 1¾ inches long and the hind or back tracks are 2 inches long.

Nine-banded armadillos are medium-size mammals covered with an armor made of plates that sit under their skin. Most times, you can count the nine bands, but there may be fewer or more on the body. Armadillos have short legs, a snout and tongue, hairless ears, and tough claws. Their underside is hairy and paler than the dark-brown-to-black upper body.

Did you know?

The raccoon is great at catching fish and other aquatic animals, such as mussels and crawfish. They are also excellent swimmers, but they apparently avoid swimming because the water makes their fur heavy. Raccoons can turn their feet 180 degrees; this helps them when climbing, especially when going headfirst down trees.

Size Comparison   Most Active   Track Size   Hibernates

3"

Northern Raccoon

Procyon lotor

Size: 24–40 inches long; weighs 15–28 pounds

Habitat: Woody areas, grasslands, suburban and urban areas, wetlands, and marshes

Range: They are found throughout Texas and the US; they are also found in Mexico and southern Canada.

Food: Eggs, insects, garbage, garden plants, berries, nuts, fish, carrion, small mammals, and aquatic invertebrates like crawfish and mussels

Den: Raccoon dens are built in hollow trees, abandoned burrows, caves, and human-made structures.

Young: 2–6 young (kits) are born around March through July. They are born weighing 2 ounces, are around 4 inches long, and are blind with lightly colored fur.

Predators: Coyotes, foxes, bobcats, humans, and even large birds of prey

Tracks: Their front tracks resemble human handprints. The back tracks sort of look like human footprints.

The northern raccoon has dense fur with variations of brown, black, and white streaks. It has black, mask-like markings on its face and a black-and-gray/brownish ringed tail. During the fall, it will grow a thick layer of fat to stay warm in the winter.

Did you know?

Otters are good swimmers and can close their nostrils while diving. This allows them to dive for as long as 8 minutes and to depths of over 50 feet. Otter fur is the thickest of all mammal fur. River otters have an incredible 67,000 hairs for every square centimeter!

Size Comparison   Most Active   Track Size

3"

Northern River Otter

Lontra canadensis

Size: 29–48 inches long; weighs 10–33 pounds

Habitat: Lakes, marshes, rivers, and large streams; suburban areas

Range: Otters can be found throughout most of the state; they are found across much of the US, except parts of the Southwest and portions of the central US.

Food: Fish, frogs, snakes, crabs, crawfish, mussels, birds, eggs, turtles, and small mammals. They sometimes eat aquatic vegetation too.

Den: They den in burrows along the river, usually under rocks, riverbanks, hollow trees, and vegetation.

Young: 2–4 young (pups) are born between November and May. Pups are born with their eyes closed. They will leave the area at around 6 months old and reach full maturity at around 2 or 3 years.

Predators: Coyotes, bobcats, bears, and dogs

Tracks: Their feet have nonretractable claws and are webbed.

Northern river otters have thick, dark-brown fur and a long, slender body. Their fur is made up of two types: a short under-coat and a coarse top coat that repels water. They have webbed feet and a layer of fat that helps keep them warm in cold water.

Did you know?

All ocelots have a different coat pattern, and the right side and left side of the body even have different coat patterns. It is estimated that there are less than 100 ocelots left in the US.

Size Comparison   Most Active   Track Size

2"

Ocelot

Leopardus pardalis

Size: 29–39 inches long; weighs 6–34 pounds

Habitat: Tropical rainforests, savannas, grasslands, and forests

Range: They are found from southern Texas to Argentina in South America.

Food: Rabbits, rodents, snakes, fish, frogs, lizards, and birds

Den: Utilizes tree branches or hollowed logs

Young: 1–4 kittens (mostly only 1) are born after a 79–82-day pregnancy. The kits are born with their eyes closed. They have their spots at birth, but they have a gray coat instead of the tan-and-brown coat. They can hunt at around 8 months and reach maturity within 20 months for females and 30 months for males.

Predators: Birds of prey and large cats

Tracks: Paws have four toes on both sets of feet. Front tracks are about 2 inches long and wide, and hind tracks are just under 2 inches wide.

Adult ocelots are brown to tan with hues of yellow. They have black-and-dark-brown spots that are shaped like doughnuts. The spots are dark tan in the middle. They have two face stripes that run from the cheeks through the eyes and over the back of the head. Their eyes are outlined in white, and they have rings on the end of their tail with stripes or bands at the base.

Did you know?

The pronghorn is the fastest land animal in North America. It can reach speeds of 60 miles per hour and jump over 20 feet in distance. The pronghorn is only found in North America. Though it looks similar to an antelope, it is not related. They are more closely related to giraffes!

Size Comparison   Most Active   Track Size

2¾"

Pronghorn

Antilocapra americana

Size: 4½ feet long; 3½ feet to shoulder; weighs 90–150 pounds

Habitat: Grasslands, shrublands, mixed-grass prairies, brushlands, and deserts

Range: The pronghorn can be found throughout much of the western United States, down into Mexico, and northward into southern Canada. In Texas, they can be found throughout central and western parts of the state.

Food: They are herbivores that eat grasses and sagebrush.

Den: No den; will bed in grass and use tall grass to hide young (fawns)

Young: Usually give birth to 1–2 fawns. They are able to stand within a few hours. The fawns will join the herd when they are about a week old and begin grazing when they are 3 weeks old. Fawns stay with their mother for about a year until they become independent.

Predators: Mountain lions, wolves, coyotes, bears, and eagles

Track: Front tracks are about 3¼ inches long, while the hind tracks are about 2¾ inches long.

Pronghorns are reddish tan to brown in color. They have a white rump, belly, chest, and cheeks. The inside of their legs is also white. Males have a black mask that extends down the face from their eyes to their nose. Males have large horns that curve inward. Females have smaller horns that are usually straight; they do not have black markings on their face.

Did you know?

Ringtails are also called civet cats, ringtail cats, and miner's cats, although they are not related to cats. They are related to raccoons! Their ankles can rotate 180 degrees, which allows them to go headfirst down a cliff or tree.

Size Comparison   Most Active   Track Size 1—1½"

Ringtail

Bassariscus astutus

Size: 24 inches long (half is tail); weighs 1½–2 pounds

Habitat: Canyons, rocky outcrops, deserts, woodlands, montane forests (forests in mountains), and shrublands

Range: They are found in the southwestern US to Texas and in northern Mexico. In Texas, they can be found throughout most of the state besides the panhandle and southwestern area.

Food: They are omnivores that eat fruit, insects, birds, flowers, small mammals, carrion (dead animals), seeds, amphibians, grains, bird eggs, reptiles, and nuts.

Den: Dens are usually in hollow trees, rock crevices, or boulder piles. They will also den in human structures. Dens are usually lined with grasses, moss, or leaves.

Young: Young are born blind and naked. Their eyes do not open until around day 30 or so when they start to eat solid food. They are weaned from milk around 2½ months. At around 10 months, they will reach reproductive maturity.

Predators: Bobcats, coyotes, and great horned owls

Tracks: Front feet are 1–1¾ inches long and 1¼–1½ inches wide. Hind feet are 1–1½ inches long and ¾–1¼ inches wide. Tracks have five toes.

Ringtails have a catlike body that is yellowish gray to black on their back and buffy gray on their belly. They have large ears, a pointed muzzle, and long whiskers. Their face has a black-to-brown-patterned mask with white-to-buffy eye rings. They have a long, buffy-colored tail that is separated by seven black rings.

Did you know?

Skunks help farmers! They save farmers money by feeding on rodents and insects that destroy crops. When skunks spray, they can aim really well! When threatened, a skunk will aim its tail towards the threat and spray a stinky musk into the target's face or eyes.

Size Comparison   Most Active   Track Size   Hibernates

   1½"

48

Striped Skunk

Mephitis mephitis

Size: 17–30 inches long; weighs 6–13 pounds

Habitat: Woodlands, prairies, and suburban areas

Range: Found throughout Texas; they can be found throughout the US and into Canada and the northern parts of Mexico.

Food: They are omnivores that eat eggs, fruits, nuts, small mammals, carrion (dead animals), insects, amphibians, small reptiles, and even garbage.

Den: Skunks prefer short and shallow natural dens, or dens abandoned by other animals, but will dig dens 3–6 feet long and up to 3 feet deep underground. Dens have multiple hidden entrances, and rooms are usually lined with vegetation.

Young: They have 4–5 young (kits) that are blind at birth; at around 3 weeks they gain vision and the ability to spray.

Predators: Raptors and large carnivores

Tracks: Their front feet have five long, curved claws used for digging; the hind foot also has five toes and is longer and skinnier than the front foot.

The striped skunk is a cat-size, nocturnal (active at night) mammal with black fur and two white stripes that run the entire length of the body. The stripe pattern is usually distinctive to each skunk.

Did you know?

The swift fox is one of North America's smallest native canids (member of the dog family), and it is slightly bigger than the kit fox. The swift fox gets its name due to its ability to run up to 25 miles per hour.

Size Comparison

Most Active

Track Size

1½"

Swift Fox

Vulpes velox

Size: 23–34 inches long; weighs 4–7 pounds

Habitat: Hillsides, prairies, deserts, ranchlands, and plains

Range: They can be found in western Canada and down through the Great Plains of the United States. In Texas, they can be found in the panhandle portion, which is a third of the state.

Food: Small mammals, fruit, amphibians, grains, berries, fish eggs, carrion (dead animals), reptiles, birds, insects, grasses, seeds, and nuts

Den: Dens are made in open prairies in sandy soils; they often construct their own but will also use dens made by other animals. Dens have multiple entrances and are at least 1 meter (about 3 feet) underground.

Young: 3–6 pups are usually born after a 50–60-day pregnancy. They will emerge from the den about a month later. Pups are born with eyes closed; they will open around 10–15 days after birth. Both parents care for the young, and pups are weaned (stop drinking milk) around 6–7 weeks. Males will reach reproductive maturity in their first winter and females usually in their second winter.

Predators: Coyotes, raptors, and badgers

Tracks: Both tracks are about 1½ inches long with 4 toes.

Swift foxes' fur is tannish orange with salt-and-pepper color on their back, sides, and legs. Their chest, belly, and the inside of their legs are white. In the summer, they have shorter fur that is a deeper red in color.

Did you know?

The opossum is the only marsupial native to the US. Marsupials are a special group of animals that are most well-known for their pouches, which they use to carry their young. When frightened, young opossums will play dead (called playing possum) and adults will show their teeth and hiss or run away.

Size Comparison Most Active Track Size 2½"

Virginia Opossum

Didelphis virginiana

Size: 22–45 inches long; weighs 4–8 pounds

Habitat: Forests, woodlands, meadows, and suburban areas

Range: They are found throughout Texas; they are found throughout the eastern US, Canada, and also in Mexico and Costa Rica.

Food: Eggs, small mammals, garbage, insects, worms, birds, fruit, and occasionally small reptiles and amphibians

Den: They den in hollow trees, abandoned animal burrows, and buildings.

Young: A litter of 6–20 young (joeys) are born blind and without fur; their limbs are not fully formed. Young will climb from the birthing area into the mother's pouch and stay until 8 weeks old; they then alternate between the mother's pouch and her back for 4 weeks. At 12 weeks they are independent.

Predators: Hawks, owls, pet cats and dogs, coyotes, and bobcats

Tracks: The front feet are 2 inches long and around 1½ inches wide and resemble a child's hands; the hind feet are 2½ inches long and around 2¼ inches wide; they have fingers in front with a fifth finger that acts as a thumb.

The Virginia opossum has long gray-and-black fur; the face is white, and the tail is pink to gray and furless. Opossums have long claws.

Did you know?
The white-nosed coati is not a raccoon, but it is in the same family. Coatis will sometimes travel over a mile in a day in search of food, often using their tail to aid in balance.

Size Comparison

Most Active

Track Size 2¼–3"

White-nosed Coati

Nasua narica

Size: 25 inches long; weighs 5½–15 pounds

Habitat: Grasslands, open forests, mountainous forests, woody canyons, and tropical woodlands

Range: They can be found from South America northward through Central America and Mexico into Texas, New Mexico, and Arizona. In Texas, they are found in the southern portion of the state.

Food: Insects, frogs, small mammals, lizards, and fruit

Den: They sleep in the tops of trees; females will build a much more robust nest in a treetop to have kits.

Young: Usually 2–7 kits are born with their eyes closed after a 2½-month pregnancy. Young open eyes at around day 11 and are weaned at around 4 months. They reach reproductive maturity at around 2 years for females and 3 years for males.

Predators: Large cats, birds of prey, humans, foxes, and snakes

Tracks: Front tracks are 2¼–3¼ inches long and 1¼–2 inches wide. Rear feet are 2¼–3 inches long and 1⅜–2 inches wide.

Coatis have small heads with a long, pointed snout or nose. They have small ears and a long tail. They have sharp claws and sport a black- or brownish-and-white mask around their eyes and nose. They have brown-to-burnt-red fur with a mixture of white and yellow on their back. Their underside is lighter brown to tannish in color. Males are larger than females.

Did you know?

When they first emerge, a deer's antlers are covered in a special skin called velvet. Deer can run up to 40 miles per hour and can jump over 8 feet vertically (high) and over 15 feet horizontally (across).

Size Comparison   Most Active   Track Size

White-tailed Deer

Odocoileus virginianus

Size: 4–6 feet long; 3–4 feet tall at front shoulder; weighs 114–308 pounds

Habitat: Forest edges, brushy fields, wooded farmlands, prairies, and swamps

Range: They are found throughout Texas and throughout the US, except for much of the Southwest; they are also found in southern Canada and into South America.

Food: Fruits, grass, tree shrubs, nuts, and bark

Den: Deer do not den but will bed down in tall grasses and shrubby areas.

Young: Deer usually give birth to twins (fawns) that are 3–6 pounds in late May to June. The fawns are born with spots; this coloration helps them hide in vegetation. Young become independent at 1–2 years.

Predators: Wolves, coyotes, bears, bobcats, and humans

Tracks: Both front and hind feet have two teardrop- or comma-shaped toes.

Crepuscular (active at dawn and dusk), white-tailed deer have big brown eyes with eye rings and a long snout with a black, glossy nose. The males have antlers, which fall off each year. All deer have a white tail that they flash upward when alarmed. Deer molt or change fur color twice a year. They sport rusty-brown fur in the summer; in early fall, they transition to winter coats that are grayish brown in color.

Did you know?

The American kestrel is the smallest species of falcon not only in the US but in all of North America! It's also the most common falcon of North America.

Nest Type   Most Active

American Kestrel

Falco sparverius

Size: 8½–12¼ inches long; wingspan of 20 inches; weight: 2¾–6 ounces

Habitat: Cities, suburbs, forests, and open areas such as meadows, grasslands, deserts, parks, and farm fields

Range: They can be found throughout Texas year-round; throughout most of North America except the extreme north of Canada and Alaska.

Food: Grasshoppers, dragonflies, small birds, lizards, and mice; sometimes snakes, bats, and squirrels

Nesting: Nest in cavities that are made by other birds like woodpeckers, in human-made and natural crevices like tree hollows, and in crevices of rock formations

Nest: They do not use nesting materials but will make a small depression if material is already present.

Eggs: 4–5 yellowish-to-white or burnt-red-brown eggs, 1–1½ inches long and 1 inch wide

Young: Chicks hatch 25–33 days after laying and will leave the nest around 30 days later. Chicks hatch with pink skin and little down feathers.

Predators: Snakes; large birds of prey, like hawks, owls, and crows; bobcats, skunks, and other mammals

Migration: Not a migrant in Texas

Kestrels sport a rusty-brown, spotted back. Their tail has a black band that stretches across it. Females have brown-to-reddish wings, and the males have grayish-blue wings. Both males and females have black lines under their eyes that resemble mascara or makeup running down their face.

Did you know?

The bald eagle is an endangered species success story! The bald eagle was once endangered due to a pesticide called DDT that weakened eggshells and caused them to crack early. Through the banning of DDT and other conservation efforts, the bald eagle population recovered, and it was removed from the Endangered Species List in July of 2007.

Nest Type   Most Active   Migrates

Bald Eagle
Haliaeetus leucocephalus

Size: 3½ feet long; wingspan of 6½–8 feet; weighs 8–14 pounds

Habitat: Forests and tree stands (small forests) near river edges, lakes, seashores, and wetlands

Range: They are a nonbreeding resident throughout Texas, with populations in the east being year-round residents; they are found throughout much of the US.

Food: Fish, waterfowl (ducks), rabbits, squirrels, muskrats, and deer carcasses; will steal food from other eagles or osprey

Nesting: Eagles have lifelong partners that begin nesting in fall, laying eggs between November–February.

Nest: They build a large nest out of sticks, high up in trees; the nest can be over 5 feet wide and over 6 feet tall, often shaped like an upside-down cone.

Eggs: 1–3 white eggs

Young: Young (chicks) will hatch at around 35 days; young will leave the nest at around 12 weeks. It takes up to 5 years for eagles to get that iconic look!

Predators: Few; collisions with cars sometimes occur.

Migration: Many migrate to Texas during the nonbreeding season of winter and will travel north during the spring.

Adult bald eagles have a dark-brown body, a white head and tail, and a golden-yellow beak. Juvenile eagles are mostly brown at first, but their color pattern changes over their first few years. A bald eagle can use its wings as oars to propel itself across bodies of water.

61

Did you know?

Brown pelicans are the only species of pelican in the United States that dives from the sky to catch food. Sometimes they dive from over 55 feet above the water. The pelican's beak system (beak and pouch) can hold an incredible amount of water, up to 3 gallons, and lots of fish!

Nest Type   Nest Type   Most Active

Brown Pelican
Pelecanus occidentalis

Size: 3½–4½ feet long; wingspan of 5¾–6½ feet; weighs 5¾–12 pounds

Habitat: Estuaries, coastal and inland areas, mangroves

Range: Brown pelicans can be found along much of North America's coast. In Texas, they are statewide along the coast and inland areas during nonbreeding season.

Food: Carnivores that mostly eat fish, as well as amphibians, eggs, crustaceans, and other birds

Nesting: March to April; pelicans engage in a courtship display.

Nest: The male selects the nest site and the female builds the nest on the ground or in a tree. Nests on the ground are usually depressions or scrapes that are lined with plants. Nests in trees are usually platforms made of sticks lined with plants. Nesting takes places in colonies with other seabirds.

Eggs: 1 brood of 2–4 chalky- or milky-white eggs

Young: Both parents incubate the nest for 28–30 days. Young fledge around 63–75 days. Birds are mature after 3–4 years.

Predators: Brown pelicans have no natural predators, but sometimes chicks and eggs are predated by gulls, skunks, raccoons, and pet dogs and cats.

Migration: Resident who does not migrate

Juvenile pelicans are mostly brown. In breeding season, adults are mostly brown with a white head with a pale-to-medium-yellow hue on top and pink skin around the eyes. The neck area is dark burgundy; the sides of the neck have white lines that outline the pelican's gular pouch (the flap on the beak). The nonbreeding adults are more drab. The female is smaller than the male.

Did you know?

Burrowing owls are fossorial, meaning that they live and/or spend most of their day underground. They will sometimes mimic rattlesnakes when threatened, by hiding in a burrow and making rattling and hissing sounds. They like to decorate their mounds with scat, or poop, from mammals. It is believed that the scat helps to attract insects to eat and to hide the scent of the owl's young.

Nest Type   Most Active   Migrates

Burrowing Owl
Athene cunicularia

Size: 7½–11 inches long; wingspan of 20–22 inches; weighs 5–6 ounces

Habitat: Savanna forest, urban and suburban areas, farmlands, shrublands, prairies, deserts, and mountains

Range: They can be found from southern Canada down into Mexico and as far east as Minnesota and Texas. In Texas, they can be found year-round in ¾ of the state and in northern Texas during the breeding season.

Food: Carnivores; mostly insects and rodents, but also amphibians, reptiles, birds, and rarely seeds and fruit

Nesting: March to April

Nest: Nests in burrows usually made by other animals. The male will line the nesting burrow with plants, feathers, scat, and sometimes trash.

Eggs: 4–12 white eggs often tinted the color of the dirt

Young: Owlets hatch 3–4 weeks after laying. Within 4 weeks, they are able to fly short distances and explore areas outside of the burrow. They will receive care for another 1–3 months until they can hunt.

Predators: Snakes, pet cats and dogs, foxes, skunks, hawks, falcons, weasels, and other owl species; humans play a heavy role in displacement and loss of habitat.

Migration: Northern populations will migrate, while populations in the southern part do not.

Burrowing owls are small, brown owls adorned by white spots of various sizes on their back. They have a white or creamy belly with brown bars. They have large yellow eyes with thick white eyebrows and throat.

Did you know?

Common grackles are tough birds who will steal worms from American robins. They also have a tool built into their beak! The hardened area on the inside of their upper beak allows them to saw open acorns. They have learned to use ants as a type of pesticide through a process called anting. During this process, ants crawl over the body of the grackle and release an acid that help get rid of parasites on the bird.

Nest Type	Most Active	Migrates

Common Grackle

Quiscalus quiscula

Size: 11–13½ inches long; wingspan of 14¼–18 inches; weighs 2½–5 ounces

Habitat: Open woodlands, marshes, farm fields, forest edges, meadows, suburbs, and parks

Range: They can be found from Canada down into Texas and eastward to Florida; their range extends north to Maine and as far west as Montana. They can be found throughout much of Texas.

Food: Salamanders, fish, crustaceans, corn, seeds, rice, acorns, insects, spiders, frogs, and other birds

Nesting: March to July; the female chooses the nest site.

Nest: A cup nest is built, usually in a tree but sometimes in cacti and other plants like cattails.

Eggs: 1–7 light-blue, white, dark-brown, or grayish eggs are laid with spots of brown on them.

Young: Young hatch 2–3 weeks after laying with eyes closed and some brownish down. They fledge 10–17 days after hatching but often remain with their parents for 1–2 days longer.

Predators: Pet cats, raccoons, hawks, owls, squirrels, and snakes

Migration: They do not migrate in much of the state; in the northwestern corner, they are breeding residents, and nonbreeding in the southwestern portion.

Common grackles are large blackbirds. The males are larger than females. Both males and females are iridescent, but the females are less shiny or glossy overall. From a distance, they appear to be black. Adults have yellow eyes, while the juveniles have dark eyes and are dark brown.

67

Did you know?

The crested caracara is actually a falcon! While other falcons will make a scrape on the ground or use an old nest built by other birds, the crested caracara is the only falcon that collects materials to build a nest.

Nest Type   Most Active

Crested Caracara

Caracara plancus

Size: 19¼–22¾ inches long; wingspan of 48–49¼ inches; weighs 37–46 ounces

Habitat: Pastures, beaches, deserts, scrub areas, wetlands, grasslands, and savannas

Range: They can be seen from southern California, as far east as central Texas, and southward to Central America. There is also an isolated population in central Florida.

Food: Carnivores, they mainly eat carrion or dead animals; they will also hunt and eat live prey like insects, fish, mammals, birds, amphibians, and reptiles. Sometimes they will even dig up turtle eggs.

Nesting: November to February

Nest: Males and females work together to build a bulky nest with a shallow bowl in a tall tree, cactus, shrub, or other structure.

Eggs: 1–4 cinnamon-to-light-brown eggs with brown spots are laid per clutch.

Young: Chicks hatch 30 days after laying, helpless and covered in down. Chicks will fledge from the nest at around 40–56 days after hatching.

Predators: Young and eggs are vulnerable to raccoons and crows, while adults have few natural predators.

Migration: Do not migrate

The crested caracara is a large falcon with long orange-to-yellow legs, a black-and-white body, white neck and cheeks, orangish-yellow face, and black cap (the top of its head). Both adult males and females look the same, while juveniles are brown and white and lack the orange and yellow of the legs and facial area.

Did you know?

The double-crested cormorant does not have oil glands like other aquatic birds; this is why you will see it on a rock or a post with its wings spread: it's drying itself off. The cormorant's bill curves at the end, while the anhinga, a similar species that is often confused with a double-crested cormorant, has a pointed, straight-top bill.

Nest Type

Nest Type

Most Active

Migrates

Double-crested Cormorant

Nannopterum auritum

Size: 26–35 inches long; wingspan of 45–48½ inches; weighs 2½–3 pounds

Habitat: Freshwater lakes, rivers, swamps, coastal waters

Range: They can be found across North America. In Texas, they are found during migration in the north and northwest parts of the state, and in the south, they can be found during the nonbreeding season.

Food: They are carnivores that eat fish, insects, snails, and crawfish.

Nesting: April to August; male chooses the nest site before finding a female. Nest in groups with other water birds

Nest: Veteran parents may repair an old nest. Otherwise, they build a new nest on the ground or in a tree. Nests are made of sticks and lined with grass. Nests can be as wide as 3 feet and over 1½ feet tall.

Eggs: On average, 4 light-bluish-white eggs are laid at a time.

Young: Young chicks (shaglets) usually hatch in 25–28 days; they can swim immediately after hatching.

Predators: Eggs are vulnerable to raccoons, gulls, jays, foxes, and coyotes. Adults and chicks are preyed on by coyotes, foxes, raccoons, eagles, and great horned owls.

Migration: They migrate south in winter.

Adults have black feathers and topaz-colored eyes, with an orange bill, throat, and face area; they have black feet that are webbed like a duck's. The tail is short. During breeding season, adults may have a "double crest" of black feathers or sometimes white, depending on the location. This is where they get their name. Young are all brown or black.

Did you know?

The great blue heron is the largest and most common heron species. A heron's eye color changes as it ages. The eyes start out gray but transition to yellow over time. Great blue herons swallow their prey whole.

Nest Type

Most Active

Great Blue Heron

Ardea herodias

Size: 3–4½ feet long; wingspan of 6–7 feet; weighs 5–7 pounds

Habitat: Lakes, ponds, rivers, marshes, lagoons, wetlands

Range: They can be found throughout Texas, as well as the entirety of the United States and down into Mexico.

Food: Fish, rats, crabs, shrimp, grasshoppers, crawfish, other birds, small mammals, snakes, and lizards

Nesting: May to August

Nest: 2–3 feet across and saucer shaped; often grouped in large rookeries (colonies) in tall trees along the water's edge. Nests are built out of sticks and are often located in dead trees more than 100 feet above the ground; nests are used year after year.

Eggs: 3–7 pale bluish eggs

Young: Chicks will hatch after 28 days of incubation; young will stay in the nest for around 10 weeks. They reach reproductive maturity at just under 2 years.

Predators: Eagles, crows, gulls, raccoons, bears, and hawks

Migration: Year-round resident that does not migrate

The great blue heron is a large wading bird with blue and gray upper body feathers; the belly area is white. They have long yellow legs that they use to stalk prey in the water. Great blue herons are famous for stalking prey at the water's edge; their specially adapted feet keep them from sinking into the mud!

Did you know?

A great horned owl can exert a crushing force of over 300 pounds with its talons. Despite its name, the great horned owl doesn't have horns at all. Instead, the obvious tufts on its head are made of feathers. Scientists aren't sure exactly how the tufts function, but they may help them stay hidden.

Nest Type   Most Active

Great Horned Owl
Bubo virginianus

Size: Up to 23 inches long; wingspan of 45 inches; weighs 3 pounds

Habitat: Woods; swamps; desert edges; as well as heavily populated areas such as cities, suburbs, and parks

Range: They are found throughout Texas and the continent of North America.

Food: They eat a variety of foods, but mostly mammals. Sometimes they eat other birds as well.

Nesting: They have lifelong partnerships, with nesting season starting in early winter; egg-laying starts in mid-January to February.

Nest: Nests are found 20–50 feet off the ground. They tend to reuse nests from other raptors or hollowed-out trees.

Eggs: The female lays 2–4 whitish eggs. Eggs are incubated for around 30 days.

Young: Young can fly at around 9 weeks old. The parents care for and feed young for several months.

Predators: Young owls are preyed upon by foxes, coyotes, bears, and opossums. As adults, they are rarely attacked by other birds of prey, such as golden eagles and goshawks.

Migration: Great horned owls are not regular migrators, but some individuals will travel south during the winter.

They are bulky birds with large ear tufts, a rusty brown-to-grayish face with a black border, and large bright eyes. The body color tends to be brown; the wing pattern is checkered with an intermingled dark brown. The chest and belly areas are light brown and have white bars.

Did you know?

The greater roadrunner can run over 15 miles per hour! It is so quick that it can grab dragonflies and hummingbirds from mid-air! Its quick speed also allows it to hunt and eat rattlesnakes.

Nest Type

Most Active

Greater Roadrunner

Geococcyx californianus

Size: 20½–21¼ inches; wingspan of 19¼ inches; weighs 17¾–19 ounces

Habitat: Scrubby habitats, deserts, brushlands, grasslands, and forest edges

Range: They can be found across the western US. In Texas, they are found statewide as year-round residents.

Food: Snakes, rodents, insects, scorpions, lizards, small birds, and sometimes fruits and seeds

Nesting: March to late-October

Nest: They build their nests in dense brush, cacti, or trees. Nests are platforms made of sticks and lined with grass, feathers, and leaves.

Eggs: 3–5 white-to-light-yellow eggs that sometimes have brown or gray stains, usually 1–2 clutches per year

Young: 19–20 days after laying, the chicks hatch with eyes closed and with white down and black skin. They will fledge from the nest at around 20 days. They reach reproductive maturity at around 2–3 years old.

Predators: Coyotes, hawks, raccoons, and pet cats

Migration: They do not migrate.

Roadrunners are medium-size, slender birds with a tan-and-brown body. Their chest and underside are streaked with black and brown. Their crown or top of the head is black with small spots of white and paler browns. They have dark wings that are highlighted by white. They have a long tail and legs.

Did you know?

Green jays have learned to use tools. They will a use a stick to get under lose bark and eat the exposed insects. Green jays can mimic just like blue jays; they will sometimes mimic hawks to scare away other birds so that they can swoop down and eat the prey that is left behind.

Nest Type   Most Active

Green Jay

Cyanocorax yncas

Size: 11½ inches long; wingspan of 15 inches; weighs 2¼–4 ounces

Habitat: Woodlands, citrus orchards, thickets, scrubby areas, and parks

Range: They can be found in areas of northern South America, Mexico, and Texas. They are found in southern Texas as year-round residents.

Food: Omnivores, they eat insects, spiders, eggs, small lizards, seeds, and other birds.

Nesting: Late March to mid-July

Nest: The male and female select the nest site together. A cup-shaped nest is built about 8½ feet off the ground in dense or brush vegetation; nests are around 8½–8¾ inches wide and 4 inches tall, with the inside of the cup being 3½ inches wide and 2½ inches deep.

Eggs: Usually 4 pale-grayish-to-greenish-white oval eggs are laid per year.

Young: Around 20 days after laying, the chicks hatch naked and relying on the parents. Both parents feed the young. Chicks will leave the nest at around 1½ months after they hatch and usually stay in the parents' territory for about 1 year.

Predators: Birds of prey like hawks and owls

Migration: Does not migrate

They have a brilliant green upper body and a lighter yellow-to-green underside. They sport a rich blue crown, throat, and area around the eye. They are communal birds who usually travel in flocks.

Did you know?

Downy woodpeckers are the smallest woodpecker species in North America. Hairy woodpeckers can hear insects traveling under the tree bark. Downy woodpeckers have a built-in mask, or special feathers, near their nostrils that helps them to avoid breathing in wood chips while pecking.

Nest Type   Most Active

Hairy/Downy Woodpecker

Leuconotopicus villosus/Dryobates pubescens

Size: Hairy: 7–10 inches long; wingspan of 13–16 inches; weighs 3 ounces. Downy: 5½–7 inches long; wingspan of 10–12 inches; weighs less than an ounce

Habitat: Forested areas, parks, woodlands, and orchards

Range: Hairy: in much of the US, and eastern Texas and a small corner of the western tip. Downy: throughout much of northern and eastern Texas and across the US.

Food: Hairy: beetles, ants, caterpillars, fruits, and seeds. Downy: beetles, ants, galls, wasps, seeds, and berries

Nesting: Hairy: March to June. Downy: January to March

Nest: In both woodpecker species, pairs will work together to create a cavity. Both parents also help to incubate eggs.

Eggs: Hairy: 3–7 white eggs. Downy: 3–8 white eggs

Young: Hairy woodpeckers' eggs will hatch 2 weeks after being laid and then fledge (develop enough feathers to fly) after another month. Downy woodpeckers' eggs will hatch after about 12 days and fledge 18–21 days after hatching. Both species hatch blind and featherless.

Predators: American kestrels, snakes, sharp-shinned hawks, pet cats, rats, squirrels, and Cooper's hawks

Migration: Woodpeckers are mostly year-round residents.

Hairy woodpeckers and downy woodpeckers look strikingly similar with their color pattern. One way to distinguish them is to look at the size of the body and bill. The downy woodpecker is smaller than the hairy woodpecker and has a shorter bill. If you look at the tail feathers of the two species, you will also see that the hairy woodpecker does not have black spots, while the downy's tail does.

Did you know?

When viewed straight-on, the yellow portion on the mallard's bill resembles a cartoon dog's head. Most domesticated ducks share the mallard as their ancestor. Mallard feathers are waterproof; they use oil from the preen gland beneath their feathers to help aid in repelling water. Mallards are the most common duck in the United States and Texas.

Nest Type	Most Active	Migrates

Mallard

Anas platyrhynchos

Size: 24 inches long; wingspan of 36 inches; weighs 2½–3 pounds

Habitat: Lakes, ponds, rivers, and marshes

Range: They are found throughout Texas as year-round residents in the northern and eastern parts of the state and nonbreeding residents in the south; the population stretches across the United States and Canada into Mexico and as far up as central Alaska.

Food: Insects, worms, snails, aquatic vegetation, sedge seeds, and grasses

Nesting: April to August

Nest: The nest is constructed on the ground, usually near a body of water.

Eggs: 9–13 eggs

Young: Eggs hatch 26–28 days after being laid. The ducklings are fully feathered and have the ability to swim at the time of hatching. Ducklings are cared for until they're 2–3 months old and reach reproductive maturity at 1 year old.

Predators: Humans, crows, mink, coyotes, raccoons, and snapping turtles

Migration: After breeding season, many birds migrate south; some may stay if food and shelter are available.

Male mallards are gray with an iridescent green head with a tinge of purple spotting, a white line along the collar, rusty-brown chest, yellow bill, and orange legs and feet. Females are dull brown with a yellow bill, a bluish area near the tail, and orange feet.

Did you know?

Cardinals are very territorial. A cardinal will sometimes attack its own reflection, thinking that another cardinal has entered its territory. The early bird gets the worm, and cardinals are some of the first birds active in the morning.

Nest Type

Most Active

Northern Cardinal

Cardinalis cardinalis

Size: 8–9 inches long; wingspan of 12 inches

Habitat: Hardwood forests, urban areas, orchards, backyards, and fields

Range: They are found throughout much of Texas, as well as the eastern and midwestern parts of the United States.

Food: Seeds, fruits, insects, spiders, and centipedes

Nesting: March to August

Nest: The cup-shaped nest is built by females in thick foliage, usually at least 1 foot off the ground. It can be 3 inches tall and 4 inches wide.

Eggs: The female lays 2–5 off-white eggs with a variety of colored speckles.

Young: About 2 weeks after eggs are laid, chicks hatch with their eyes closed and mostly naked, aside from sparsely placed down feathers.

Predators: Hawks, owls, and squirrels

Migration: Cardinals do not migrate.

Northern cardinal males are bright-red birds with a black face. Females are a washed-out red or brown. Both males and females have a crest (tuft of feathers on the head), an orange beak, and grayish legs. Cardinals can be identified by their laser-gun-like call.

Did you know?

Northern mockingbirds get their name from their ability to mimic or "mock" sounds of other birds, organisms, and even machines. They can sing 40 to more than 200 songs, depending on their region. Mockingbirds will bravely defend their nests from larger birds like raptors. When danger is present, mockingbirds can form an allegiance with neighbors to protect the shared area.

Nest Type Most Active

Northern Mockingbird

Mimus polyglottos

Size: 8–10 inches long; wingspan of 12–14 inches; weighs 1½–2 ounces

Habitat: Hardwood forests, urban areas, parks, orchards, backyards, and fields

Range: They are found throughout Texas, as well as the rest of the United States; in the northern US, they are migrants.

Food: Omnivore that feeds on seeds, fruits, insects, earthworms, and sometimes lizards

Nesting: Spring to early summer

Nest: The cup-shaped nest is built by both males and females, with the male doing most of the building. The nest is composed of twigs and lined on the inside with dead leaves, grass, moss, and manmade materials.

Eggs: 3–5 blue-to-green eggs speckled with brownish red

Young: About 2 weeks after the mother lays the eggs, chicks hatch. They're born nearly naked and with their eyes closed.

Predators: Pet cats, crows, snakes, blue jays, hawks, owls, and squirrels

Migration: Does not migrate

Mockingbirds are medium-size grayish songbirds. They have a white belly and dark-gray wings with a bold white patch. Mockingbirds have a long dark-gray tail with bright-white outer feathers.

Did you know?

The osprey is nicknamed the "fish hawk" because it is the only hawk in North America that mainly eats live fish. An osprey will rotate its catch to put it in line with its body, pointing headfirst, which allows for less resistance in flight as the air travels over the fish.

Nest Type

Most Active

Migrates

Osprey
Pandion haliaetus

Size: 21–23 inches long; wingspan of 59–71 inches; weighs 3–4½ pounds

Habitat: Near lakes, ponds, rivers, swamps, and reservoirs

Range: They are breeding, nonbreeding, and migratory residents in all of Texas and throughout the US.

Food: Feeds mostly on fish; they sometimes eat mammals, birds, and reptiles if there are few fish.

Nesting: For ospreys that migrate, egg-laying happens in April and May. The female will take on most of the incubation of the eggs, as well as the jobs of keeping the offspring warm and providing protection.

Nest: Platform nests are constructed out of twigs and sticks. Nests are constructed on trees, snags, or human-made objects like cellular towers and telephone poles.

Eggs: The mother lays 1–3 cream-colored eggs with splotches of browns and pinkish reds.

Young: Chicks hatch after around 36 days and have brown-and-white down feathers. Ospreys fledge around 50–55 days after hatching and will receive care from parents for another 2 months or so.

Predators: Owls, eagles, foxes, skunks, raccoons, and snakes

Migration: Ospreys migrate south to wintering areas in the fall.

spreys are raptors, and they have a brown upper body and hite lower body. The wings are brown on the outside and white n the underside, with brown spotting and streaks toward the dge. The head is white with a brown band that goes through e eye area, highlighting the yellow eyes.

Did you know?

The red-tailed hawk is the most abundant hawk in North America. The red-tailed hawk's scream is the sound effect that you hear when soaring eagles are shown in movies. Eagles do not screech like hawks, so filmmakers use hawk calls instead! Red-tailed hawks can't move their eyes, so they have to move their entire head in order to get a better view around them.

Nest Type

Most Active

Red-tailed Hawk

Buteo jamaicensis

Size: 19–25 inches long; wingspan of 47–57 inches; weighs 2½–4 pounds

Habitat: Deserts, woodlands, grasslands, and farm fields

Range: They are found throughout Texas and throughout North America.

Food: Rodents, birds, reptiles, amphibians, bats, and insects

Nesting: Hawks mate for life; nesting starts in March.

Nest: Both the male and female help build a large cup-shaped nest, which can be over 6 feet high and 3 feet across; the nest is made of sticks and branches; nests are built at forest edges mostly in the crowns of trees, but hawks will also nest on windowsills and other human-made structures.

Eggs: 1–5 eggs; the insides of eggs are a greenish color.

Young: They start to fly after 5–6 weeks, and it takes around 10 weeks for the hatchlings to leave the nest.

Predators: Great-horned owls and crows

Migration: Does not migrate

Red-tailed hawks are named for their rusty-red tails! They have brown heads and a chest that's cream to light brown with brown streaking in the form of a band. Red-tailed hawks are highly territorial, and throughout the day they will take to the air to look for invaders.

Did you know?

Red-winged blackbirds are one of the most abundant songbirds in the United States. Sometimes their winter roost (colony) can have several thousand to up to a million birds. In many areas, red-winged blackbirds are considered a pest because of their love of grain and seeds from farm fields. In others, they are welcomed because they eat insects that are considered pests to farmers.

Nest Type

Most Active

92

Red-winged Blackbird

Agelaius phoeniceus

Size: 7–9½ inches long; wingspan of 13 inches; weighs 2 ounces

Habitat: Marshes, lakeshores, meadows, parks, and open fields

Range: They are throughout Texas as year-round residents. Their range extends from central Canada through the US and into Mexico.

Food: Dragonflies, spiders, beetles, snails, seeds, and fruits

Nesting: February to August

Nest: Female builds a cup from plant material.

Eggs: 3–4 eggs that come in a variety of colors, from pale blue to gray with black-and-brown spots or streaks

Young: Chicks hatch blind and naked after around 12 days of incubation. Hatchlings will leave the nest after 12 days but will continue to receive care for another 5 weeks.

Predators: Raccoons, mink, marsh wrens, and raptors

Migration: Texas populations do not migrate.

Red-winged blackbird males are a sleek black with an orangish-red spot that overlays a dandelion-yellow spot on the wings. Females have a combination of dark-brown and light-brown streaks throughout the body. Male red-winged blackbirds spend much of the breeding season defending their territory from other males and attacking predators or anything else that gets too close to the nest.

Did you know?

Spoonbills have feathers on their head until they reach maturity around 3 years or so; that's when they get the iconic bald head. Spoonbills also hatch with a straight bill, which later changes to the famous spoon-like shape as they get older. Their nostrils are located high up on their bill, near the eyes. This enables them to breathe while the rest of the bill is underwater.

Nest Type

Most Active

Roseate Spoonbill

Platalea ajaja

Size: 28–34 inches long; wingspan of 47–50 inches; weighs 2½–4 pounds

Habitat: Shrubby coastal areas, marshes, bays, swamps, mangroves, and mudflats

Range: Found throughout coastal Texas and southeastern US coasts

Food: Mostly carnivorous; feeds on crustaceans, shrimp, aquatic insects, amphibians, and smaller fish

Nesting: Nesting takes place in trees and shrubs near water in colonies with other wading birds. Both parents will incubate the eggs.

Nest: Large and cup shaped, made of branches and stems. Males collect the nest material and the females build the nest in high shady areas.

Eggs: 2–5 off-white-to-green eggs with brown spots

Young: Chicks are born with eyes closed and covered in down feathers, 20–23 days after laying. They leave the nest at 35 days and are independent at 7 weeks.

Predators: Eggs and chicks are the most vulnerable to raccoons, coyotes, and hawks. As adults, alligators, coyotes, and humans can be predators (due to illegal hunting).

Migration: Year-round resident of Texas

Roseate spoonbills are large, pink wading birds. Both male and female adults have a featherless greenish-gray head. The neck, back, and breast are covered in white feathers. The rest of the body is covered in rose-colored feathers. During breeding season, they sport a deep hot-pink-colored shoulder patch. Juveniles are a paler pink and have a head covered with feathers.

Did you know?
The sandhill crane is the most abundant crane species in the world. They are not afraid to defend themselves when threatened. They will use their feet and bill to ward off predators, often stabbing attackers with their bill. Sometimes sandhill cranes will travel 500 miles in one day to find food.

Nest Type

Most Active

Migrates

Sandhill Crane

Grus canadensis

Size: 3½–4 feet long; wingspan of 6–7 feet; weighs 7½–10 pounds

Habitat: Grasslands, savannas, and farm fields

Range: Breeding resident in western North America. They can be found during migration in many states. They are found across much of Texas as nonbreeding residents and migratory residents in the east and northwestern corner of the state.

Food: Berries, insects, snails, amphibians, and small mammals, as well as food crops like corn

Nesting: Nonmigratory populations will lay eggs from December to August, while populations that migrate will nest between April and May.

Nest: Both adults build the cup-shaped nest using vegetation from nearby areas.

Eggs: Up to 3 pale-brownish-yellow eggs with brown spots

Young: Chicks are born with the ability to see and walk. Chicks become independent at around 9 months and will start breeding between 2 and 7 years.

Predators: Coyotes, raccoons, ravens, great horned owls, and humans

Migration: Cranes arrive in late March to early May and migrate south from September to December.

The sandhill crane is a large bird with gray-to-brownish feathers with a white face and ruby-red crown. They are commonly seen in large groups in fields.

Did you know?
Scissor-tailed flycatchers get their name from their long tail feathers, which resemble scissors at various stages of flying and perching. When flying, they look like open scissors, and when perching, the feathers resemble closed scissors.

Nest Type

Most Active

Migrates

Scissor-tailed Flycatcher
Tyrannus forficatus

Size: 8¾–14½ inches long; wingspan of 5¾–6 inches; weighs 1¼–2 ounces

Habitat: Semi-open areas like grasslands, shrublands, farmlands, and savannas

Range: They can be found in the western to midwestern United States, southward to Mexico, and as far east as Louisiana. In Texas, they are found statewide during the breeding and migration seasons.

Food: Insects, spiders, some fruits, and berries

Nesting: April to August

Nest: Nests are built by females. They are made with natural materials like Spanish moss, cotton, plant stems, flowers, as well as human-made materials.

Eggs: 3–5 eggs whitish-to-cream-colored eggs with splotches of brown, red, and purple

Young: Chicks hatch naked with brown-and-red-hued skin and a little down. Both parents bring food to nestlings. Young will leave the nest about 14–16 days after hatching.

Predators: Mostly birds of prey, though reptiles may eat eggs and hatchlings

Migration: Migrates from Central America during the breeding seasons and returns south in the fall

They have white-gray bodies with charcoal wings; their tail feathers are black and white. They have pink-to-orangish-pink patches on their underwings and sides. The males have larger tails than the females. Juveniles' tails are not as long as adults' and are less forked.

Did you know?

Turkeys sometimes fly at night, unlike most birds, and land in trees to roost. Turkeys have some interesting facial features; the red skin growth on a turkey's face above the beak is called a snood, while the growth under the beak is called a wattle. Wild turkeys can have more than 5,000 feathers.

Nest Type

Most Active

Wild Turkey

Meleagris gallopavo

Size: 3–4 feet long; wingspan of 5 feet; males weigh 16–25 pounds; females weigh 9–11 pounds

Habitat: Woodlands and grasslands

Range: Found throughout Texas. They also can be found in the eastern US and have been introduced in many western areas of the country.

Food: Grain, snakes, frogs, insects, acorns, berries, and ferns

Nesting: April to September

Nest: The nest is built on the ground using leaves as bedding, in brush or near the base of trees or fallen logs.

Eggs: 10–12 tan eggs with very small reddish-brown spots

Young: Poults (young) hatch about a month after eggs are laid; they will flock with the mother for a year. When young are still unable to fly, the mom will stay on the ground with her poults to provide protection and warmth. When poults grow up, they are known as a hen if they are female, or a gobbler or tom if they are male.

Predators: Humans, foxes, raccoons, owls, eagles, skunks, and fishers

Migration: Turkeys do not migrate.

A wild turkey is a large bird that is dark brown and black with some iridescent feathers. Males will fan out their tail to attract a mate. When threatened, they will also fan out their tail and rush the predator, sometimes kicking and puncturing prey with the spurs on their feet.

Did you know?

Wood ducks will "mimic" a soccer player when a predator is near their young: they flop! Female wood ducks will fake a broken wing to lure predators away from their young. Wood duck hatchlings must jump from the nest after hatching to reach the water. They can jump 50 feet or more without hurting themselves.

Nest Type   Most Active   Migrates

Wood Duck

Aix sponsa

Size: 15–20 inches long; wingspan of 30 inches; weighs about 1 pound

Habitat: Swamps, woody ponds, and marshes

Range: They are mostly nonbreeding residents throughout Texas, but they can be found in a section of eastern Texas as year-round residents and a small tip of northern Texas as breeders; they are also in the eastern US, southern Mexico, the Pacific Northwest, and on the West Coast.

Food: Fruits, nuts, and aquatic vegetation, especially duckweed, sedges, and grasses

Nesting: March to August

Nest: Wood ducks use hollow trees, abandoned woodpecker cavities, and human-made nesting boxes.

Eggs: 8–15 off-white eggs are laid once a year. Sometimes females will lay eggs in another female's nest; this process is called egg dumping.

Young: Eggs hatch about a month after being laid. Chicks will leave the nest after a day and fly within 8 weeks.

Predators: Raccoons, mink, fish, hawks, snapping turtles, owls, humans, and muskrats

Migration: They are nonbreeding residents in much of Texas but migrate to breeding areas during the fall.

Wood duck males have a brightly colored crest (tuft of feathers) of iridescent (shimmering) green, red, and purple, with a mahogany (brown) upper breast area and tan bottom. Males also have red eyes. Females are brown to gray. Wood ducks have strong claws that enable them to climb up trees into cavities.

Did you know?

Alligator snapping turtles are the largest freshwater turtle species in North America! They can weigh over 200 pounds. Being that big, it has a bite force of 1,000 pounds. That's not the only amazing thing about their mouth; an alligator snapping turtle has a built-in "lure" (or skin protrusion) on its tongue that acts like bait to attract prey.

Most Active

Hibernates

Alligator Snapping Turtle

Macrochelys temminckii

Size: Male: 31 inches long; weighs 150–200 pounds.
Female: 20–22 inches long; weighs 60–63 pounds

Habitat: Rivers, streams, lakes, bayous, and swamps

Range: Alligator snapping turtles are endemic, or only found in the US. They are found along the eastern portion of Texas that borders Louisiana, Arkansas, and Oklahoma.

Food: Carnivores, they feed on aquatic animals like fish, crawfish, clams, mussels, and some plant materials, as well as birds and snakes.

Mating: April to June; must travel to find mates

Nest: Female travels away from water sources on land and digs a nest in sand or dirt.

Eggs: 1 clutch per year of around 10–60 spherical, whitish eggs with a leathery shell

Young: Eggs will hatch around 100 days after laying. Nest temperature determines sex at hatching: male turtles develop in cooler nest temperatures and females develop at warmer nest temperatures. They are fully independent at hatching, do not receive any care from parents, and reach reproductive maturity around ages 11–13.

Predators: Raccoons, birds, otters, and fish will prey on eggs and juveniles. Adults are hunted by humans.

They have a spiked, dark-brown carapace. Alligator snapping turtles have three rows of raised scutes that resemble spikes on their carapace (back shell) that are brown to greenish gray. The plastron (bottom shell) is lighter than the carapace. They have a large triangular or spade-shaped head with a hooked beak. **105**

Did you know?

The male alligator does not have vocal cords. The growling or roaring sound that males make in order to attract females comes from the alligator filling its lungs with air and exhaling. Alligators sometimes trick birds into landing or flying close to them by placing sticks and vegetation on their head; birds looking for nesting material will fly and try to retrieve the sticks and be met by the gator's mouth.

Most Active

American Alligator

Alligator mississippiensis

Size: 8–16 feet long; weighs up to 1,000 pounds

Habitat: Freshwater ponds, coastal areas, rivers, swamps, and brackish water (mix of fresh and saltwater)

Range: In Texas, they can be found in the coastal areas of the eastern border to the south-central portion that touches Mexico. They are native to the southeastern US.

Food: Snakes, fish, birds, mammals, insects, and even fruit

Mating: Starts in spring and goes until May or early June. Mating takes place at night. Males have multiple mates.

Nest: Nests are made of plant material and can be 3 feet tall by 7 feet wide. Eggs are covered with vegetation.

Eggs: 35–50 white eggs

Young: Eggs hatch about 2 months after laying. Hatchling sex is temperature dependent; nest temperatures below 88 degrees or above 90½ degrees usually produce females, and temperatures of 89½ to around 90½ degrees usually produce males. They reach independence at 1 year and reproductive age at around 10 years. Hatchlings form pods or groups and alert others to nearby danger by making clicking noises.

Predators: Humans; as juveniles: birds, snakes, bobcats, raccoons, otters, large fish, and older alligators

The American alligator is a thick-bodied reptile with short legs. It has a wide U-shaped snout. The body has thick skin in colors of black to brownish gray; the tail is thick and muscular, and the underside is white. Hatchlings are striped for the first several months. If the water freezes, alligators will bury themselves in mud and stick their snouts out for several days.

Did you know?

Terrapins are the only turtles in the world that live in brackish water (mix of salt and freshwater). They have special glands called lachrymal salt glands that help them get rid of salt in the body. Terrapins have powerful jaws that help them in eating different types of animals with shells, like snails and clams. Diamondback terrapins get their name from the diamond-shape markings on their carapace (top shell).

Most Active   Hibernates

108

Diamondback Terrapin

Malaclemys terrapin

Size: Male: 5½–6 inches long; weighs ½ pound.
Female: 11–12 inches long; weighs 1½ pounds

Habitat: Coastal areas like estuaries, tidal creeks, salt marshes, mangroves, and lagoons

Range: They can be found as far north as Massachusetts and as far south as the Florida Keys, and westward into Texas. In Texas, they are found along coastline, in barrier beaches, salt marshes, tidal flats, and streams and creeks containing brackish water.

Food: Fish, crabs, mussels, marine snails, insects, carrion (dead things), clams, and other mollusks

Mating: May to June

Nest: Nests are usually in sand dunes or scrub vegetation.

Eggs: Female will lay 2 or 3 clutches a year. Clutches range from 4–23 eggs, but usually 5–10 pinkish-white eggs.

Young: Hatchlings usually emerge 2–3 months after laying and are fully independent at hatching. Like other turtles, terrapins have temperature-dependent sex determination. Females mature around year 7, but due to their smaller size, males mature around 2 or 3 years.

Predators: Wild hogs, herons, raccoons, humans, crabs, rats, gulls, crows, mink, and foxes

The diamondback terrapin is a species of turtle native to the eastern and southern United States and Bermuda. The shell appears wedge-shaped and can vary from brown to gray. The body can be gray, brown, yellow, or white. All have a unique pattern of wiggly, black markings or spots on their body and head. Diamondback terrapins have large, webbed feet and are very strong swimmers.

Did you know?

When they are in danger or threatened, eastern collared lizards will stand up and run on their hind legs. They can reach speeds over 15 miles per hour to escape predators.

Most Active

Eastern Collared Lizard

Crotaphytus collaris

Size: 8–14 inches long; weighs 2 to 4½ ounces

Habitat: Rocky canyons, cliffs, shrublands, flat canyon bottoms, woodlands, areas with exposed bedrock, and gullies

Range: They can be found in northern Mexico and several western states. In Texas, they can be found in the central and western portions of the state.

Food: Small snakes, grasshoppers, moths, spiders, beetles, and other lizards

Mating: Mid-May to early June

Nest: Burrow dug beneath a large rock

Eggs: 4–10 eggs per clutch are laid within 20 days after breeding; may lay a second clutch.

Young: Hatchlings hatch 2–2½ months after being laid. They experience a rapid growth and are large enough to mate at around 1 or 2 years. Hatchlings' sex is dependent on egg temperature during incubation.

Predators: Coyotes, bobcats, lizards, birds, pet cats, snakes, foxes, and hawks

The eastern collared lizard sports a large head and long tail. Breeding males are various shades of tans with bright blues and greens and a bright-yellow head. They have irregular spots or blotches across their body. Females are brownish to green in color. Females that are carrying eggs have spots on their bodies that fade after they have laid their eggs. Both males and females have one irregular black line that sits just behind the head, with a second broader and wider line that extends across the neck and stops at the top of the front limbs. Juveniles are yellow with a collar that resembles the adults. They have a series of orange-to-yellowish blotches down their body.

Did you know?

The eastern newt starts its life in the water and then lives on land as a juvenile before returning to live out the rest of its life in the water as an adult. Some newts will skip the juvenile stage and change straight into an adult. Eastern newts have a toxin that they release through their skin that makes potential predators sick. The bright-orange color of an eastern newt acts as a warning system to would-be predators that they taste bad or are toxic.

Most Active   Hibernates

Eastern Newt (Red-spotted Newt)

Notophthalmus viridescens

Size: 3–5 inches long; weighs less than a dime

Habitat: Streams, marshes, lakes, ponds, and in woodlands

Range: They are found from New England and the Atlantic Coast to the west as far as eastern Texas.

Food: Aquatic insects, snails, worms, amphibians, and fish eggs

Mating: Breeding season for the eastern newt starts in the winter and finishes in early spring.

Nest: No true nest; eggs are laid underwater.

Eggs: Females lay eggs in the spring, in still or quiet water. Eggs attach to underwater vegetation. Females lay 200–400 eggs, providing no form of care.

Young: The larvae hatch around 3–8 weeks after eggs are laid. Larvae transform into efts (juveniles) by the end of summer. Efts live on land for 1–3 years. When mature, they return to the water for the remainder of their lives.

Predators: Fish, birds, insects, amphibians, and reptiles

The eastern newt goes through three life stages. It has a fully aquatic or water-living stage as a larva. During this stage, it has gills and a flat tail. In the next stage (the juvenile stage), it lives on land. This stage of life is called the red eft stage. During this stage, it sports rough, bright-red skin with red spots and has a rounded tail. The last stage is the adult stage, where it has a brownish-yellow-to-olive-brown color on the upper half of the body, red spots outlined by black circles, and a yellow underside with black spots on it.

Did you know?

Females can produce over 45,000 eggs, but the average is usually around 10,000. The temperature can affect the rate that Great Plains toads go through metamorphosis; if the temperature is too warm and the water that they are living in is in risk of drying out, they undergo the process faster. The males let out a long, loud trill during the breeding season to attract mates.

Most Active

Hibernates

Great Plains Toad

Anaxyrus cognatus

Size: 2–3½ inches long; weighs 2 ounces

Habitat: Plains, grasslands, sandhills, farm areas, and semi-desert shrublands

Range: They are found in portions of southern Canada and several states of the Midwest and southwestern United States. They are found in the panhandle and western corner of Texas.

Food: Worms, beetles, ants, and other insects

Mating: Breeds mainly in late spring and early summer, in pools, ponds, and reservoirs

Nest: No nest is built; females use shallow bodies of water (no more than 12 inches deep) to lay eggs in.

Eggs: Females lay around 11,000 eggs at one time. Eggs are laid in a row of long strings that are nestled in two layers of jelly. Females can lay over 20,000 eggs in one season.

Young: Tadpoles hatch 2–7 days after being laid. Tadpoles metamorphose or change into small toads in about 2 months. They reach maturity within 3–5 years.

Predators: Raccoons, water bugs, fish, hognose snakes, grackles, and skunks

Great Plains toads can be identified by their round snout, dry warty skin, and large eyes that sit on the top of their head. They have two ridges or crests above each eye that combine and make a bump on their snout called a "boss." They come in various colors of creams to tans, with blotches of darker tans, browns, and greens covering their body. They have a large parotid gland behind each eye. Their underside is light brown to cream with no spots.

Did you know?

Unlike other sea turtles, green sea turtles are mostly herbivores (plant eaters). They eat algae and other plants, which gives their fat and muscles a greenish tint, leading to their name! Loggerheads get their odd name because sailors originally mistook them for logs or tree trunks.

Most Active

Green Sea Turtle (GST)/
Loggerhead Sea Turtle (LST)

Chelonia mydas / Caretta caretta

Size: GST: 3–4½ feet long; weighs 250–500 pounds.
LST: 2½–3½ feet long; weighs 200–375 pounds

Habitat: Coastal areas and open ocean

Range: LST: Found on the Texas coast. GST: Found around the world where the water is warm enough

Food: GST: Seagrass and algae. LST: Crabs, jellyfish, conches, fish

Mating: (GST) June to September and (LST) May to August. Mating takes place every 2–4 years.

Nest: GST: A cavity about 30 inches deep. Both species nest above the surf line (where waves crash) on beaches. Females can lay multiple batches of eggs a season and usually will lay a new nest after about 14 days or so. LST: A cavity around 18 inches deep.

Eggs: GST: 100-130 Ping-Pong-ball-size eggs. LST: 100-130 eggs

Young: After 2 months of incubating, hatchlings emerge and immediately travel toward the ocean.

Predators: Feral hogs, sharks, raccoons, dogs, humans, crows, birds, fish, ants, crabs, cats, coyotes, foxes, bears, and skunks

Green sea turtles are the second-largest sea turtle (the leatherback is bigger). Their shell is dark brown to olive colored with a yellow-to-pale plastron (underside). Loggerheads have a distinctive large head and heart-shaped carapace (shell) that ranges from brown to red. The underside is paler and yellow to off-white.

117

Did you know?

Kemp's ridley sea turtles are the smallest sea turtles in the world. They are the only sea turtles that nest during the day and one of two sea turtle species that nest in large groups called arribadas.

Most Active

Kemp's Ridley Sea Turtle

Lepidochelys kempii

Size: 27–32 inches long; weighs 80–100 pounds

Habitat: Coastal areas and open ocean

Range: Found on the Texas coast in the Gulf of Mexico and along the eastern US coast in the northern Atlantic Ocean.

Food: Mainly crabs; also feed on jellyfish, mollusks or shellfish, and fish

Mating: April to July; mating takes place every 2–4 years

Nest: Nests are above the surf line (where waves crash) on sand dunes. Females can lay multiple nests a season. Nesting takes place during the daytime.

Eggs: 100–110 Ping-Pong-ball–size eggs

Young: Hatchlings hatch 50–60 days after laying. Hatchlings crawl to the sea and spend 2–10 years in the open ocean. They return to shallower waters near shore to develop into adults. They are reproductively mature at around 10–13 years.

Predators: Feral hogs, sharks, raccoons, dogs, humans, crows, birds, fish, ants, crabs, cats, coyotes, foxes, bears, and skunks

Kemp's ridley sea turtles are greenish to gray on their upper body with a paler cream-to-yellow stomach. They have a hooked beak mouth and a circular carapace (top of shell). They have one claw on each front flipper and one or two claws on each back flipper. The hatchlings are black to charcoal gray.

Did you know?

Plains hognose snakes are venomous! But luckily, their venom is not harmful to us. Hognoses' fangs have a dual purpose: to inject venom into prey and to deflate frogs or toads who may puff their bodies up. The hognose uses some interesting techniques to ward off would-be predators. First, the snake will flatten its head to look like a cobra. Then, if that doesn't work, it will play dead by flipping over and letting its tongue hang out of its mouth.

Most Active   Hibernates

Plains Hognose Snake

Heterodon nasicus

Size: 15–40 inches long; weighs 60–120 grams or about 5 ounces

Habitat: Prairies, neighborhoods, pastures, canyons, floodplains, scrub brush, farm fields, deserts, and montane woodlands

Range: From southern Canada down into western Minnesota, southward to eastern New Mexico. In Texas, they can be found along the northwestern and central parts of the state.

Food: Small birds, turtles, lizards, smaller snakes, mammals, eggs, ants, beetles, and grasshoppers

Mating: Late spring to early summer

Nest: Females dig out nests in loose sandy soil and lay eggs; sometimes, eggs are laid in a row in a tunnel instead of clustered together.

Eggs: 2–24 oval eggs that are white or cream in color. Eggs for this species have smooth, leathery shells.

Young: Hatchlings are more brightly colored than adults. They reach maturity at around 2–3 years for females and 1–2 years for males.

Predators: Hawks, crows, and coyotes

Plains hognose snakes are small, thick-bodied snakes with an upturned or shovel-shaped snout. They come in various shades of brown and tan with 20–55 darker brown blotches that run down their back. Along their sides, they have two alternating rows of spots that travel the length of their body. They have several dark lines that run the length of their face from corner to corner; often, one line runs across both eyes, framing them like a mask.

Did you know?
The snapping turtle's sex is determined by the temperature of the nest! Nest temperatures that are 67–68 degrees produce females, temperatures in the range between 70 and 72 degrees produce both males and females, and nests that are 73–75 degrees will usually produce all males.

Most Active

Snapping Turtle, Common

Chelydra serpentina

Size: 8–16 inches long; weighs 10–35 pounds

Habitat: Rivers, marshes, and lakes; can be found in areas that have brackish water (freshwater and saltwater mixture)

Range: They are found throughout the state of Texas; also found in the eastern US and southern Canada.

Food: These omnivores (eat both plants and animals) eat frogs, reptiles, snakes, birds, small mammals, and plants.

Mating: April to November are the breeding months; lays eggs during June and July

Nest: Females dig a hole in sandy soil and lay the eggs into it.

Eggs: 25–42 eggs, sometimes as many as 80 or more

Young: Like sea turtles, snapping turtles have temperature-dependent sex determination (TSD), meaning the temperature of the nest determines the sex of the young. Hatchlings leave the nest between August and October. In the North, turtles mature at around 15–20 years, while southern turtles mature around 12 years old.

Predators: Raccoons, skunks, crows, dogs, and humans

The snapping turtle's carapace (top shell) is dark green to brown and usually covered in algae or moss. The plastron (or bottom of the shell) is smaller than the carapace. They are crepuscular animals that are mostly active during the dawn and dusk hours. Young turtles will actively look for food. As adults, they rely heavily on ambushing to hunt; they bury themselves in the sand with just the tip of their nose and eyes showing.

Did you know?

Speckled kingsnakes are also called the "salt-and-pepper snakes." They get their name due to their large size and the fact that they eat snakes that are not only longer than them, but also those that are venomous. They have some immunity to (can't get hurt by) venom.

Most Active

Hibernates

Speckled Kingsnake

Lampropeltis holbrooki

Size: 36–48 inches long; can reach up to 72 inches; weighs 3–5 pounds

Habitat: City areas, wetlands, grasslands, woodlands, forests, floodplains, fields near streams, shrublands, and shortgrass prairies

Range: They can be found from Iowa to states of the Gulf Coast and west from Texas to eastern New Mexico, Colorado, and throughout most of Kansas. In Texas, they can be found throughout the central and eastern portions of the state.

Food: They are carnivores that eat rodents, birds, lizards, snakes, eggs, and amphibians.

Mating: Breed in spring once they come out of hibernation

Nest: No nest; they lay eggs under rocks, stumps, logs, or dying plant materials.

Eggs: 6–23 eggs are laid at a time.

Young: Snakelets hatch 8–12 weeks after laying. They are 7–9 inches long and reach adulthood 4–6 months after hatching.

Predators: Red-tailed hawks, pet cats, great horned owls, golden eagles, and other snakes, including other speckled kingsnakes

Speckled kingsnakes are nonvenomous snakes that have smooth scales. They have black eyes and a yellow underside with irregular black barring across the body. Their topside has a black head, body, and tail. Each black scale has a yellow spot at the front toward the center of the scale. Sometimes, the yellow spots will fuse together and form bars on the back. Males are just a little longer than females.

Did you know?

Spiny softshell turtles will bury themselves under a layer of mud at the bottom of a lake, with only their head sticking out, and catch prey as it passes by. In addition to breathing through their lungs, they can extract oxygen from the water through their skin; this aids them in being able to stay underwater for over 4 hours.

Most Active

Spiny Softshell Turtle

Apalone spinifera

Size: Females: 7–19 inches long (carapace); males: 5–10 inches long; females weigh 20–30 pounds, while males are considerably smaller.

Habitat: Sand bars, lakes, rivers, wetlands, and city areas

Range: They can be found as far north as Canada and as far south as Mexico. They can be found in South Carolina and Georgia and as far west as California. In Texas, they can be seen throughout, mostly in the eastern and central parts of the state.

Food: Aquatic insects, fish, snails, tadpoles, and crawfish

Mating: Mating takes place in the spring.

Nest: Eggs are buried in a flask-shaped chamber that is around 4–10 inches deep, along rivers, in sand bars, or on loose soils on banks.

Eggs: 4–38 white eggs are laid per clutch.

Young: Young hatch between 65–85 days after laying. Young turtles are about 1½ inches long at hatching. While in other turtle species the sex of hatchlings is determined by temperature, in spiny softshell turtles, it is determined by genetics. Females become reproductively mature at around ages 8–9, while males become mature at around age 4.

Predators: Raccoons, herons, large fish, and foxes

Spiny softshell turtles are brown-to-olive, flat-shaped turtles with dark spots on their back and limbs. They have a long, snorkel-like nose and webbed feet. The front of the carapace has spines and bumps. Females are larger than males, but males have longer and thicker tails. Their shell is leathery and lacks scutes or scales. The underside, or plastron, is cream or yellow.

Did you know?

When threatened, the Texas banded gecko will freeze and mimic a scorpion by holding its tail above its body and moving it side to side; if that's doesn't work, it will detach its tail and run away, leaving the predator to go after its flopping tail.

Most Active

Texas Banded Gecko

Coleonyx brevis

Size: 4–5 inches long; weighs around 2 grams

Habitat: Dry rocky areas, deserts, and rock piles

Range: They can be found in a band from the northeastern corner of Mexico through coastal Texas to southern New Mexico.

Food: They eat insects, spiders, and other soft-bodied organisms called arthropods.

Mating: March to April

Nest: Females lay eggs under flat rocks.

Eggs: 1–2 smooth, white-shelled, oblong or oval-shaped eggs

Young: Young hatch about 2 months after laying, looking like adults with brown bands that fade into lighter yellow as they age. Young reach reproductive maturity shortly after they hatch.

Predators: Snakes

Texas banded geckos have brown bodies striped with alternating bands of brown and yellow or cream and sometimes pink. They are slim in frame with slender legs. Their tail is equal to their body length. They have big eyes with vertical pupils and eyelids.

Did you know?

Horned lizards are named for the crown of horns on their head. Although sometimes called horned toad, horned frog, or horny toad, they are not amphibians, but reptiles. When threatened, horned lizards will inflate themselves with air to look larger. If this technique doesn't work, they can spray blood from the corners of their eyes, confusing predators and allowing them to escape.

Most Active   Hibernates

Texas Horned Lizard

Phrynosoma cornutum

Size: 2½–4 inches long; weighs 1–3½ ounces

Habitat: Plains, grasslands, open dry areas, prairies, and sandy areas

Range: They are found in the south-central United States to northern Mexico. In Texas, they are mostly statewide.

Food: Harvester ants make up most of their diet, but they will eat other ants and insects, as well as spiders.

Mating: Mid-April to mid-June after hibernation

Nest: Females dig a nest in loose soil or under large rocks.

Eggs: Females lay 14–37 eggs in late May, June, or July.

Young: Eggs hatch within 1–2 months after laying. They are independent at hatching and will reach reproductive maturity at around 2 years.

Predators: Lizards, ground squirrels, hawks, coyotes, snakes, roadrunners, and pet cats and dogs

Texas horned lizards are small but stocky (wide and flat-bodied). Two rows of enlarged fringed scales run down both sides of their body. Their limbs have pointed scales. They have multiple horns on their head, with two of them longer than the others. Most horned lizards have a light-tan or buffy-colored line that extends down their back. They have two large dark spots behind their head, with more dark markings along their back. Their underside is tan to cream-colored.

Did you know?

The Texas toad is the state amphibian of Texas. It is one of the most common toads of the southern United States. During the summer when it is hot, the Texas toad will cool off by digging into the ground and burying itself in mud or soil.

Most Active   Hibernates

Texas Toad

Anaxyrus speciosus

Size: 2–3½ inches long; weighs 22¾–34½ ounces

Habitat: Wetlands, grasslands, open woody areas, lands with sandy soil, and holes or tunnels made by small mammals

Range: They are found in northern Mexico, Oklahoma, and New Mexico. In Texas, they are found in most of the state.

Food: Insects such as beetles, ants, flies, and moths; they also eat centipedes and millipedes, as well as spiders.

Mating: April to September

Nest: Eggs are laid in pools of shallow water after rain, usually around the base of vegetation.

Eggs: Eggs are brown and have yellow spots with a jelly layer surrounding them.

Young: Tadpoles hatch around 2–3 days after laying. It takes around 2 weeks–2 months for them to develop. They leave the pond as juveniles and reach reproductive maturity in 1–2 years.

Predators: Grackles, turtles, snakes, and, as tadpoles, beetle larvae

Texas toads are round-bodied amphibians with grayish-to-brown skin. Their skin is bumpy with warts. They have brown and yellowish-green spots on their back. Males are usually smaller than females.

Did you know?

A rattlesnake will rattle the base of its tail to warn would-be predators; it can move its rattle back and forth 60 or more times a second. Rattlesnakes are venomous (their bites inject toxin), so do not go near one or try to pick one up! Instead, leave it alone so it can help people by munching on rodents and other pests. Rattlesnakes are "pit vipers," snakes that have a special body part that helps them "see" heat.

Most Active   Hibernates

Safety Note: These snakes are venomous (toxic). If you see one, observe or admire it from a distance.

Western Diamondback Rattlesnake

Crotalus atrox

Size: 3–5 feet long; weighs 3–14 pounds

Habitat: Rocky hillside, grassy plains, coastal areas, deserts, and forests

Range: They are found in the southwestern states of the US from California to Texas and the northern half of Mexico. In Texas, they are found almost statewide besides the northern and eastern parts.

Food: Carnivores, they feed on mice, rats, rabbits, gophers, ground-dwelling birds, and lizards.

Mating: Spring following hibernation

Nest: Gives live birth in a burrow or hollow log

Eggs: No eggs; young are birthed live.

Young: 10–12 young are born at a time. Young will stay with the mother for a few hours and scatter to find shelter and live independently. Young have fangs and venom at birth. They reach reproductive maturity at around 3 years.

Predators: Coyotes, eagles, hawks, foxes, kingsnakes, bobcats, and roadrunners

The western diamondback rattlesnake is a thick snake with an arrow- or triangle-shaped head. Two diagonal lines that are dark colored run from the mouth to the eyes, as if it is wearing a mask. It has dark, diamond-shaped patterns that run down its olive-brown or tan body. The diamond pattern on its back is where it gets its name.

Did you know?

The western tiger salamander can grow up to 14 inches long and and live over 20 years! Western tiger salamanders migrate to their birthplace to breed. Tiger salamanders have a hidden weapon! They produce a poisonous toxin that is secreted or released from two glands in their tail. This toxin makes them taste bad to predators and allows them to escape.

Most Active   Hibernates

Western Tiger Salamander

Ambystoma mavortium

Size: 7–14 inches long; weighs 4½ ounces

Habitat: Woodlands, marshes, and meadows; they spend most of their time underground in burrows.

Range: They are found across much of Texas, except the eastern portion of the state; populations are found in the western United States.

Food: They are carnivores that eat insects, frogs, worms, and snails.

Mating: Tiger salamanders leave their burrows to find standing bodies of freshwater. They breed in late winter and early spring after the ground has thawed.

Nest: No nest, but eggs are joined together into one group in a jelly-like sack called an egg mass. An egg mass is attached to grass, leaves, and other plant material at the bottom of a pond.

Eggs: There are 20–100 eggs or more in an egg mass.

Young: Eggs hatch after 2 weeks, and the young are fully aquatic with external gills. Limbs develop shortly after hatching; within 3 months, the young are fully grown but will hang around in a vernal pool. Individuals living in permanent ponds can take up to 6 months to fully develop.

Predators: Young are preyed upon by diving beetles, fish, turtles, and herons. Adults are preyed upon by snakes, owls, and badgers.

Western tiger salamanders have thick black, brown, or grayish bodies with uneven spots of yellow, tan, brown, or green along the head and body. The underside is usually a variation of yellow. Males are usually larger and thicker than females.

137

Glossary

Adaptation—An animal's physical (outward) or behavioral (inward) adjustment to changes in the environment.

Amphibian—A small animal with a backbone, has moist skin, and lacks scales. Most amphibians start out as an egg, live at least part of their life in water, and finish life as a land dweller.

Biome—A part or region of Earth that has a particular type of climate and animals and plants that adapted to live in the area.

Bird—A group of animals that all have two legs and feet, a beak, feathers, and wings; while not all birds fly, all birds lay eggs.

Brood—A group of young birds that hatch at the same time and with the same mother.

Carnivore—An animal that primarily eats other animals.

Clutch—The number of eggs an animal lays during one nesting period; an animal can lay more than one clutch each season.

Crepuscular—The hours before sunset or just after sunrise; some animals have adapted to be most active during these low-light times.

Diurnal—During the day; many animals are most active during the daytime.

Ecosystem—A group of animals and plants that interact with each other and the physical area that they live in.

Evolution—A process of change in a species or a group of animals that are all the same kind; evolution happens over several generations or in a group of animals living around the same time; evolution happens through adaptation, or physical and biological changes to better fit the environment over time.

Fledgling—A baby bird that has developed flight feathers and has left the nest.

Gestation—The length of time a developing animal is carried in its mother's womb.

Herbivore—An animal that primarily eats plants.

Hibernate—A survival strategy or process where animals "slow down" and go into a long period of reduced activity to survive winter or seasonal changes; during hibernation, activities like feeding, breathing, and converting food to energy all stop.

Insectivore—An animal whose diet consists of insects.

Incubate—When a bird warms eggs by sitting on them.

Invasive—A nonnative animal that outcompetes native animals in a particular area, harming the environment.

Mammal—An air-breathing, warm-blooded, fur- or hair-covered animal with a backbone. All mammals produce milk and usually give birth to live young.

Migration—When animals move from one area to another. Migration usually occurs seasonally, but it can also happen due to biological processes, such as breeding.

Molt—When animals shed or drop their skin, feathers, or shell.

Nocturnal—At night; many animals are most active at night.

Piscivore—An animal that eats mainly fish.

Predator—An animal that hunts (and eats) other animals.

Raptor—A group of birds that all have a curved beak and sharp talons; they hunt or feed on other animals. Also known as a bird of prey.

Reptile—An egg-laying, air-breathing, cold-blooded animal that has a backbone and skin made of scales, which crawls on its belly or uses stubby legs to get around.

Scat—The waste product that animals release from their bodies; another word for it is poop or droppings.

Talon—The claw on the feet seen on raptors and birds of prey.

Torpor—A form of hibernation in which an animal slows down its breathing and heart rate; torpor ranges from a few hours at a time to a whole day. Torpor does not involve a deep sleep.

Checklist

Mammals

- [ ] American Badger
- [ ] American Beaver
- [ ] Black Bear
- [ ] Black-tailed Jackrabbit
- [ ] Black-tailed Prairie Dog
- [ ] Collared Peccary
- [ ] Coyote
- [ ] Desert Bighorn Sheep
- [ ] Eastern Fox Squirrel
- [ ] Mexican Free-tailed Bat
- [ ] Mexican Long-nosed Bat
- [ ] Mountain Lion
- [ ] Nine-banded Armadillo
- [ ] Northern Raccoon
- [ ] Northern River Otter
- [ ] Ocelot
- [ ] Pronghorn
- [ ] Ringtail
- [ ] Striped Skunk
- [ ] Swift Fox
- [ ] Virginia Opossum
- [ ] White-nosed Coati
- [ ] White-tailed Deer

Birds

- [ ] American Kestrel
- [ ] Bald Eagle
- [ ] Brown Pelican
- [ ] Burrowing Owl
- [ ] Common Grackle
- [ ] Crested Caracara
- [ ] Double-crested Cormorant
- [ ] Great Blue Heron
- [ ] Great Horned Owl
- [ ] Greater Roadrunner
- [ ] Green Jay
- [ ] Hairy/Downy Woodpecker
- [ ] Mallard
- [ ] Northern Cardinal
- [ ] Northern Mockingbird
- [ ] Osprey
- [ ] Red-tailed Hawk
- [ ] Red-winged Blackbird
- [ ] Roseate Spoonbill
- [ ] Sandhill Crane
- [ ] Scissor-tailed Flycatcher
- [ ] Wild Turkey
- [ ] Wood Duck

Reptiles and Amphibians

- [ ] Alligator Snapping Turtle
- [ ] American Alligator
- [ ] Diamondback Terrapin
- [ ] Eastern Collared Lizard
- [ ] Eastern Newt
  (Red-spotted Newt)
- [ ] Great Plains Toad
- [ ] Green/Loggerhead
  Sea Turtle
- [ ] Kemp's Ridley Sea Turtle
- [ ] Plains Hognose Snake
- [ ] Snapping Turtle, Common
- [ ] Speckled Kingsnake
- [ ] Spiny Softshell Turtle
- [ ] Texas Banded Gecko
- [ ] Texas Horned Lizard
- [ ] Texas Toad
- [ ] Western
  Diamondback Rattlesnake
- [ ] Western Tiger Salamander

The Art of Conservation®

Featuring two signature programs, The Songbird Art Contest™ and The Fish Art Contest®, the Art of Conservation programs celebrate the arts as a cornerstone to conservation. To enter, youth artists create an original hand-drawn illustration and written essay, story, or poem synthesizing what they have learned. The contests are FREE to enter and open to students in K-12. For program updates, rules, guidelines, and entry forms, visit: www.TheArtofConservation.org

The Fish Art Contest® introduces youth to the wonders of fish, the joy of fishing, and the importance of aquatic conservation. The Fish Art Contest uses art, science, and creative writing to foster connections to the outdoors and inspire the next generation of stewards. Participants are encouraged to use the Fish On! lesson plan, then submit an original, handmade piece of artwork to compete for prizes and international recognition.

The Songbird Art Contest® explores the wonders and species diversity of North American songbirds. Raising awareness and educating the public on bird conservation, the Songbird program builds stewardship, encourages outdoors participation, and promotes the discovery of nature.

Photo Credits

About the Author

Alex Troutman is a wildlife biologist, birder, nature enthusiast, and science communicator from Austell, Georgia. He has a passion for sharing the wonders of nature and introducing the younger generation to the outdoors. He holds both a bachelor's degree and a master's degree in biology from Georgia Southern University (the Real GSU), with a focus in conservation. Because he knows what it feels like to not see individuals who look like you (or come from a similar background) doing the things you enjoy or working in the career that you aspire to be in, Alex makes a point not only to be that representation for the younger generation, but also to make sure that kids have exposure to the careers they are interested in and the diverse scientists working in those careers.

Alex is the co-organizer of several Black in X weeks, including Black Birders Week, Black Mammologists Week, and Black in Marine Science Week. This movement encourages diversity in nature, the celebration of Black individual scientists, awareness of Black nature enthusiasts, and diversity in STEAM fields.

ABOUT ADVENTUREKEEN

We are an independent nature and outdoor activity publisher. Our founding dates back more than 40 years, guided then and now by our love of being in the woods and on the water, by our passion for reading and books, and by the sense of wonder and discovery made possible by spending time recreating outdoors in beautiful places. It is our mission to share that wonder and fun with our readers, especially with those who haven't yet experienced all the physical and mental health benefits that nature and outdoor activity can bring. #bewellbeoutdoors